DO WHAT YOU
BELIEVE

OR YOU WON'T BE FREE
TO BELIEVE IT MUCH LONGER

"In this book, Steve challenges each of us to live THE truth, not our truth or a version of truth. The Truth. Easier said than done. All the way through, Steve issues a clarion call to all those that wish to be more than a 'sunshine Patriot.' By the end of the book, you will not only accept Steve's solution, you will know it is our last and only chance."

—**Glenn Beck**, Radio Hall of Famer and *New York Times*
bestselling author

"Steve Deace is a hero. He has written this spectacular how-to guide for Christians to know precisely how to shine our lights brightly amidst the darkness threatening America at this crucial time!"

—**Eric Metaxas**, #1 *New York Times* bestselling author of
Bonhoeffer, If You Can Keep It, and *Is Atheism Dead*

"Two words describe this book: clarity and courage. Deace has a gift for clearing through the chaos and confusion of our day, diagnosing the problems at hand, then incisively prescribing tangible, just solutions. *Do What You Believe* offers a compelling answer to the perpetually asked question, '*But what do we do?*'"

—**Allie Beth Stuckey**, BlazeTV

"This book validates Christian activism in defense of this nation, as founded, not as a matter of partisanship, but Godly obedience. We don't love America simply because it is our country, but because it was founded on Christian principles—principles that we have largely abandoned. In these pages, my friend Steve Deace inspires and equips Christians to boldly proclaim the Gospel and to unapologetically fight to restore the extraordinary liberty tradition our founders established. We Christians must quit cowering to today's secular culture. We must lead in Christ's image, rather than follow, submissively, the forces of this world, which are being led by invisible, spiritual forces. Will we have the courage to fight for the things that matter most and please God or will we seek, instead, to please man? This book needed to be written, and God bless Steve Deace for writing it. Now, let's do our part in standing strong for Christ, for His church, and for America before it irretrievably squanders its unique historical role as a beacon of godly goodness and a shining city on a hill."

—*New York Times* bestselling author **David Limbaugh**

"Steve Deace's new book is written for Christians who care to defend themselves in post-Christian America. It is a sobering book full of good advice. Deace reminds us that, 'You are a stranger in a strange land almost everywhere you go now. But remember this: the Kingdom of God forcefully advances, and it is forceful men who lay hold of it. Not passive ones. Forceful ones.' We are called to be crusaders rather than door-mats for pagans and atheists."

—**Emerald Robinson**, Newsmax TV

"Why do Christ-followers continue to long for a country that no longer seems to exist? What can we do, going forward, to resist evil and effect change? In *Do What You Believe*, Steve Deace calls us to see ourselves 'more as pilgrims than patriots,' as he offers the Church a pathway to stand tall against the 'Spirit of the Age' while upholding the holiness of God and the character of Jesus. *Do What You Believe* will initiate an important conversation as Christians try to live bravely and proclaim boldly."

—**J. Warner Wallace**, *Dateline*-featured Cold-Case Detective, Senior Fellow at the Colson Center for Christian Worldview, and author of *Person of Interest: Why Jesus Still Matters in a World That Rejects the Bible*

This book is dedicated to all of those who let God use you to impact my life so God could then use me to impact others. May we all finish well.

A POST HILL PRESS BOOK
ISBN: 978-1-63758-257-2
ISBN (eBook): 978-1-63758-258-9

Post Hill Press
New York • Nashville
posthillpress.com

Published in the United States of America
1 2 3 4 5 6 7 8 9 10

DO WHAT YOU BELIEVE

OR YOU WON'T BE FREE TO BELIEVE IT MUCH LONGER

STEVE DEACE

POST Hill
PRESS

Table of Contents

Acknowledgments

As always, I want to thank my assistant Todd Erzen for his help editing and providing feedback on this project as it was being assembled. Todd also is responsible for the group study questions you'll "enjoy" at the end of each chapter as well, which I trust you'll find both challenging and edifying.

I also want to thank the folks at Blaze Media for allowing me to work at a platform that isn't ashamed of the name of Jesus, as well as contrarian views. There are so few platforms of significance that we can say such things about these days, so please by all means I hope each of you reading it support it if you get the chance.

This is not meant to be a humble brag, though it may come across as one, but this is the third book project I've done in just the past year. Needless to say, that pace has required some extra hours after my work on my daily show typing away on my laptop at my desk at home. I want to thank my wife, Amy, and our kids for patiently putting up with it. I promise to not write another one of these for at least a few months!

Finally, thank you to all our listeners/viewers. You're most responsible for the enormous growth of our show, as well as the shocking success of my previous work *Faucian Bargain: The Most Powerful and Dangerous Bureaucrat in American History.* I pray you'll be rewarded by what you're about to read in this one.

Introduction

"WE'RE DOING IT WRONG"

I grew up mostly in the 1980s, and one of my favorite childhood films from that era is the Michael Keaton classic *Mr. Mom*.

In the movie, Keaton's character is the proverbial fish out of water, a modern-day stranger in a strange land. He's gone from being a mover and shaker in the corporate world—the primary breadwinner for his family—to a stay-at-home dad struggling to find his purpose and maintain his identity.

Sound familiar? In many respects, Keaton's character is a metaphor for the modern American church. The positions of father and husband he still holds still pack a punch when it comes to tradition and status, but whether or not he still knows how to wield any actual influence with them within the paradigm shift his family is undergoing is up for debate. He was so used to his authority being acknowledged one particular way that now he's cut off from that original path, he believes he's less of a man.

How much money he makes, his accomplishments, and other performance-related affirmation and approval originally defined Keaton's character. However, once he loses his job he's now cast in the far more difficult role of servant-leadership. He was always daddy to his children, but now he's also their primary caregiver. And he's totally unprepared for the thanklessness of the job.

Now he does the cleaning and the shopping (including a hilarious scene where he's charged with purchasing a feminine hygiene product for his wife at the grocery store) and becomes the stay-at-home father to the kids. The tasks he's charged with now go unnoticed by everyone, including his wife, who has rejoined the workforce and is now focused on her climb up the corporate ladder.

He seeks affirmation in all the wrong places: food, soap operas, coupon poker games, and "exotic" nights on the town with the other desperate housewives in the neighborhood. None of these activities are thoroughly satisfying.

Along the way he makes several mistakes and feels more and more out of place every day. He's so out of his element he can't even manage to drop the kids off at school correctly. As he drives up to his children's school's parking lot in a pouring rain one fateful morning, the crossing guard confronts Keaton's character, pointing to a sign that indicates he's driving in the wrong direction and causing a traffic jam for the other more experienced parents.

"You're doing it wrong," she declares to Keaton.

Indeed we are.

As believers, we understand the difficulty of Keaton's transition. We are in the world, but not of it. Before we were children of God we were also motivated by the same things Keaton's character originally was: money, prestige, power, and success. Then one day we hear God's effectual call of the wild and come to Christ and worship Him as Lord and Savior.

Our previously dead in sin spirit comes alive, and suddenly the world looks completely different. To borrow a phrase from *The Matrix*, we have taken the red pill and now realize just how far down the rabbit hole goes. Slowly but surely over time our tastes change, our attitudes get adjusted, and our vision gets clearer. What we see and what we seek change.

We begin to recognize that what we once called good is really evil, we understand that what we once described as freedom is really bondage, and we have a zeal to spread that Good News to the ones around us still held captive by deception.

We search the Scriptures looking for the best ways to do that. Then Jesus presents us what are the most challenging paradoxes in the history of humanity: die to live, deny to gain, endure persecution to be blessed, and be prepared to give up everything we hold dear to follow Him.

Before we lived to indulge our own desires, but now we know our lives are not our own because we were bought at a great price. Suddenly we're to care for the least of these, when before we wanted to keep up with the Joneses. Suddenly we're told to expect opposition for doing the right thing, when before hardly anybody got in our way for doing the wrong one.

But that's okay for a while, because we now have something we never had before—joy. The joy of knowing history is headed somewhere, the joy of knowing this life isn't all there is, and the joy of knowing we're loved by our heavenly Father no matter what.

Then the honeymoon period expires, and it's time to go to work. We realize that God saved us for something more than just eternal fire insurance. We realize that He has predestined good works for us to do. Good works that would bring glory to Him. Good works that demonstrate His mercy, compassion, truth, and love. We are convinced that faith without works is dead. We feel God's call to go and serve in the arena and play our role in the redemptive process.

Once we get out and engage the world and get our hands dirty, we begin to struggle when confronted with the reality that we're fighting a lost cause by the world's standard. And the world never hesitates to tell us just how weird and naïve we really are, too. Sometimes even our closest family members and friends turn against us, and we can't figure out why that is because we're actually a kinder and more loving people than we were before.

Sure, we still say amen when the preacher says one day every knee will bow and every tongue will confess that Christ is Lord. We may even believe that to be true. But the broken road that takes us beyond belief and to conviction has a new obstacle: our own lack of real, I-know-it-in-my-gut faith.

We yearn for God to say to us one day, "Well done, good and faithful servant, enter into the joy of your master." Yet it's tough to endure till that end when we don't receive affirmation every time we take a stand for what seems like the right thing. It's tough to endure when we don't experience victory while defending Christ's honor and teachings. And that's even if we're not already discouraged to see the culture around us sink even further into the abyss.

We look to THE CHURCH (which we will capitalize in this book whenever we're addressing the universal body of believers) to provide us the means to be world-changers. But THE CHURCH is divided, and a house divided against itself cannot stand. After all, there are thousands of different denominations and sects, so who knows what the truth really is? That's not to say there aren't legitimate doctrinal reasons for splinters and schisms. I'm certainly not shy about expressing my own views on such matters. However, isn't it ironic that the *more* we schism and splinter, the *less* doctrinally aware the culture around us becomes?

In 1980, as America was attempting to recover from the societal earthquake known as the counterculture of the 1960s and the scandals and cynicism of the 1970s, the inestimable thinker and tactician Francis Schaeffer wrote *A Christian Manifesto.* He urged American Christians to renew the faithfulness, orthodoxy, and activism that inspired those original ragtag thirteen colonies, distinctly founded on Judeo-Christian tradition, to alter the course of human history.

I believe it is time for a similar call to arms before this exceptional country is lost to history on our watch. While I wouldn't presume to carry Schaeffer's jock strap, I also don't see a long line of holier and wiser alternatives offering God's people anything beyond just keep doing what we've always done, but hope/expect to see a different result this time—otherwise known as Einstein's classic definition of insanity. Therefore, after spending more than a decade in full-time activism, I'm going to give it my best shot.

If we've learned anything the past few decades it's that while voting is important, we cannot simply vote our way out of this. We're way past being a silent majority that just shows up to right the previous years of wrongs every Election Day. We're too far gone for that, I'm afraid. We live in a society that believes men can have a uterus and women are merely "birthing units."

In other words, we aren't in Kansas anymore, Toto.

Not to mention that too often the differences between the two major political parties are but pale pastels, when what is required to confront the Spirit of the Age (the term we will use in this book for the earthly manifestation of the demonic adversaries we face) is bold colors. Which is why this book will strive to be different from others you've read and tried before when it comes to its call for activism. For this book believes ultimately the problem and the solution is one and the same—**the answer is us.** The Creator is aware of the problem. That's why He put us here.

Unfortunately, today we live in a country that, while founded and inspired by Judeo-Christian teaching, is in many ways as ignorant of our ways as the natives the Pilgrims first encountered on this continent five hundred years ago. What's called "progressive" these days is often regressive and seeking to return Western civilization to a pre-Christendom view of the world. It is driven by a Spirit of the Age that casts itself in political camouflage and thus escapes direct confrontation from much of THE CHURCH, but underneath that disguise is pure paganism. Many of our elite sectors of American culture have much more in common with the Druids than the disciples.

THE CHURCH seems focused on winning souls at the expense of transforming hearts and changing minds. However, if we're really winning souls, shouldn't there be abundant evidence of transformation among the faithful? Evangelism has become a clever marketing system that is labeled successful if enough folks come through the turnstiles to answer our cattle call each Sunday morning and the on-site coffeehouse shows a profit at the end of the month. Salvation comes down to signing a decision card or tearfully giving your life to Jesus once while saying the "sinner's prayer."

The Bible isn't preached as much as Bible verses are used, sometimes out of context, to make the point of the preacher or the cuddly lesson that shows just how cutting edge and contemporary we can be. Under this model, the concept of true discipleship—or what it means to really submit to the will of Christ in our lives— is rarely addressed corporately on Sunday mornings. Instead discipleship is voluntary and requires a person to enlist in a complementary class, if one exists at all. This model relegates discipleship to a whenever-you-get-to-it program, since we can't afford to bore our modern multitudes with "useless head knowledge."

I once addressed my concerns with this approach to the lead pastor of a prominent church in my community. He responded, "We often discuss as a staff how much of that stuff our people really need to know."

You know, "stuff" like ample evidence for the authenticity of Scripture that demands a verdict, "stuff" like sanctification, and "stuff" like the proven prophecies that sets Christianity apart from every other belief system on the planet. Trite "stuff" like that. It appears the foundations of our faith that formed historic, orthodox Christianity—and forged this nation—have been relegated to "stuff" status for the social media generation.

That leaves too many of us lacking the knowledge of what we really believe and why we really believe it. We also end up lacking the knowledge of what the world believes about what we believe. This leads to a chronic lack of discernment and critical thinking, which turns us from citizens in a self-governing society into subjects of an all-powerful state.

We are the salt that has lost its flavor, and when that happens it's no longer of use to anybody except to be thrown out and trampled underfoot. Salt is an irritant, a preserver, and a cleanser for a wound so it can be treated. But all three of those characteristics bring with it some semblance of confrontation, and that doesn't fit our business model and mission statement, you know.

Then, all too often in the churches that do try and address the knowledge of the truth, they do so with little concern for the condition and frailty of the heart. They become performance-based ministries, based on how much you know and what worldly temptations you're successfully denying yourself. They live in a constant "give up–try harder" cycle, with people confessing the same sins over and over again until they get tired of the shame and just start hiding who they really are.

They place a standard on the people that is impossible to live up to without really and lovingly dealing with the pain—past, present, and future—that the people are dealing with. These ministries also pride themselves on their unwillingness to adapt with the times at all. No need for any multimedia or a change in music style, they say, because this is the way it's always been done. They think they're being steadfast in their ministry, but it's really just stubbornness. They become holy huddles, unaware or uninterested in what's going on in the culture around them.

Some of our ministries avoid engagement because it's messy and they just can't afford to get any of the world on them. They're the ones who take their talent and hide it out of an unhealthy fear of God, believing Him to be more taskmaster than Father. They think their lack of growth and generational changeover just goes to prove they're being persecuted for holding fast to the truth.

Then some of our ministries have engaged so much they seem more engaged to the world than they are the Bride of Christ. They have become so relevant that they're now relative. They almost practice a reverse snobbery, believing any acknowledgment of orthodoxy or tradition is pretentious and gets in the way of reaching out to the lost by any means necessary. They quote the Gospel of Bobby McFerrin—"Don't worry, be happy" is their mantra—more than the Gospel of Jesus Christ. The idea of suffering for what you believe is anathema, which is unfortunate since it's only proven to be the most effective method of advancing the faith.

There's a lot of talk today that America has turned its back on THE CHURCH. I think the exact opposite is true. I think America is mirroring what it sees from THE CHURCH. Why are Americans by and large lazy about their liberties, complacent instead of courageous in conviction, materialistic, disinterested in doctrine, lacking wisdom and critical-thinking skills, disengaged from one another, and plunging into sectarian balkanization? Golly, I wonder where such behaviors were learned and modeled? Turns out there's a lot to that binding and loosing thing.

Therefore, either those in THE CHURCH are not being truly transformed from the inside-out, or THE

CHURCH is permitting itself to be deformed by the Spirit of the Age from the outside-in. Both options are bad, and the end result is the same—next stop is the ash heap of history.

THE CHURCH leads in every community it's planted, but it doesn't bloom in every culture it's planted in. Sometimes it just coexists on a parallel track with the culture, and like two ships passing in the night THE CHURCH and the culture never intersect. Other times it just blends in with the culture and becomes just another institution of like-minded do-gooders who live for access, affirmation, and approval from the world so it can't afford to offend it.

It is time to stop being victims, to stop feeling helpless, and to starting doing what we believe. While we may be collectively less free than any previous generation of Americans, we're still more free than any previous era of Christendom. We still have more ability to advance the Kingdom than previous generations of believers, who had to risk their lives just to travel to the places they would later risk their lives evangelizing and discipling. History is won by those who actually show up. The truth is we have been outflanked by the Spirit of the Age because we were outworked. It wanted to hijack this culture more than we wanted to conserve it, so here we are.

But the good news is the same God who rolled the stone away is still sovereign. The Bible and the Constitution may effectively be dead letters in mainstream America, but our God specializes in resurrections. He's still eager to reward faithfulness. The harvest is still plenty, but the workers remain few.

This book is for those who hear that call to arms and respond with "here I am LORD, send me."

But before we carry on with the rest of our discussion, let's make sure our priorities are clear. We do not do this in place of the Gospel, *but because of it*. We do not fight for the culture contained within this land mass known as these United States of America in place of the Gospel, *but because of it*. We do not commit to activism in place of evangelizing the Gospel, *but because of it*.

Meaning, God commands us to be good stewards of our resources, and He has undoubtedly shed His grace on thee. Despite all the blemishes, imperfections, and injustices in our history, other than THE CHURCH itself there has been no greater force for good in this fallen world the past two hundred–plus years than these United States of America.

Our forefathers wielded the sword of righteousness against injustice, both foreign and domestic. They bled and died for this flawed vehicle of a country, believing it to be a modern-day city on a hill capable of shining a light in the darkness. They didn't get choked up seeing the colors of this flag or hearing that national anthem because of a simplistic jingoistic fervor, but because of the transcendent values and ideals those symbols represent— as well as the high cost paid to boldly proclaim them.

And guess where those transcendent values and ideals came from? From where did this unique and impactful heritage emerge?

Where the Spirit of the Lord is, there is liberty. The flame of liberty in America was lit by the blaze in the pulpit, and it will only be preserved by the same. And while the Gospel prevailed in this world long before there was an America, and it will do so long after she's gone, we cannot deny that God has chosen in His sovereignty to wield America as His sword of righteousness against evildoers. Our Creator gave our nation the privilege of being a force for good, so wouldn't it be a good thing to preserve its goodness? How does it advance the Kingdom to sit by and allow a culture inspired by God's Word to fade to black?

G. K. Chesterton once eloquently observed, "America is the only country ever founded on a creed." That creed is found in our Declaration of Independence: all men are created equal, endowed by the Creator with unalienable (preexistent, divinely given) rights, and chief among these are life, liberty, and the pursuit of happiness.

Where did the tenets of this creed come from? Where all righteous creeds originate—the laws of Nature and Nature's God. Thus, this is no different than fighting for any other principles found in God's Word. We'd find it weird or offensive if a church told us it really wasn't that important to do activism to feed the hungry, would we not? Then shouldn't we also be offended when a church tells us not to bother activating to protect innocent life and virtue? Besides, if the creed America was founded upon wasn't such a powerful force for good, then why in the world is the Spirit of the Age fighting so hard as we speak to end it?

Once more, we do not fight for these things as American believers instead of the Gospel, *but because of it.*

Who knows, though, maybe that time is past? Maybe America's run is at an end, and her ruin is at hand? Let's face it, if this is it for America as the world's superpower it's not as if it isn't deserved. We have collectively turned our backs on our heritage and thus the God from whom our rights come.

But if this is to be the end, let it not be because we passively stood by and mistakenly labeled a self-fulfilling prophecy as divine judgment. Let it not be because we dug our own graves. Let it not be because we played ourselves. If this is to be America's curtain call, let it be because God needed to judge this land to uphold His righteous character, not because it's a judgment upon the lack of character of His people.

Let us instead fight like it's up to us, but pray and worship like it's up to Him. And then, come what may, we will boldly proclaim God is good all the time, and all the time God is good—whether or not America survives.

Group Discussion Questions

1. When it is suggested to you that modern-day American Christianity might be "doing it wrong," what response does that immediately provoke from you?

2. Are there Biblical/historical parallels to those responses? Are the answers obvious, or do you see through a glass darkly in terms of how the past holds the answers for the future?

3. What is the level of guilt/complicity for our current state of affairs in the average Christian individual? The localized church? The corporate church? Where is the Spirit of the Age excused or encouraged the most?

4. What costs of correcting the problems laid out above are the biggest roadblocks to revival? What do we fear the most?

5. What is the most inspired you've ever been regarding the connection between your faith and American citizenship?

Chapter 1

FIRST WE MUST CORRECT SOME STINKIN'

THINKIN'

Before we can fully move forward into a realization of the true state of the culture we find ourselves in, and therefore the level of confrontation it will take to get it to change course, we need to remove an albatross holding us back.

In the last year or so before writing this book, I have probably received more questions and fallacies from believers around the country regarding this passage of Scripture than any other: Romans 13:1–7.

Let's take a look at what Paul says in this passage using the English Standard Version of the Bible, which is a word-for-word translation of the original text into our contemporary language:

> *Let every person be subject to the governing authorities. For there is no authority except from God, and those that exist have been instituted by God. Therefore whoever resists the authorities resists what God has appointed, and those who resist will incur*

judgment. For rulers are not a terror to good conduct, but to bad. Would you have no fear of the one who is in authority? Then do what is good, and you will receive his approval, for he is God's servant for your good. But if you do wrong, be afraid, for he does not bear the sword in vain. For he is the servant of God, an avenger who carries out God's wrath on the wrongdoer. Therefore one must be in subjection, not only to avoid God's wrath but also for the sake of conscience. For because of this you also pay taxes, for the authorities are ministers of God, attending to this very thing. Pay to all what is owed to them: taxes to whom taxes are owed, revenue to whom revenue is owed, respect to whom respect is owed, honor to whom honor is owed.

Too many believers have been taught this passage means they are to be compliant and subservient subjects of the state no matter what it demands of us. Which is ironic, given you also live in the country that fought arguably the most successful revolution in human history. Yet for the sake of argument, let's set our native land's history aside and just look at church history. If subservience is what Paul truly means here, then why did the Emperor Nero decapitate him? Why was Paul martyred?

Wouldn't the fact he was martyred at least imply that somewhere along the way Paul actually defied Nero? Surely if what Paul meant was for every citizen to become a model mascot for bowing to tyrants, he would've lived longer. Which means that somewhere along the way Nero asked something of Paul he could not give. So what was Paul's line he couldn't cross, even for the most powerful ruler in the world?

Fellow believer, we must unpack this dilemma before we take on the Spirit of the Age. For if we are not convinced we're right to do what must be done, the odds dramatically decrease we'll be successful trying to do it. There are six things Romans 13:1–7 does and doesn't say, which will help us know what every believer must understand if we're going to successfully navigate the first post-Christian generation in American history:

1. This passage does not mean do everything government tells you. And you know this by looking at how Paul himself lived out his own teaching and what happened to him as a result.

If this passage of Scripture is meant to mean unconditional allegiance to government, then Paul apparently didn't understand his own words given to him by the Holy Spirit. Because somewhere along the line he defied Nero to the point of earning his own execution.

When it was time for me to explain the Biblical principle of father/husband headship in the home to my daughters, I asked them if their mother should submit to my leadership if I decided to become a drug dealer. After all, I'm the head of the home, right? And elsewhere in the Bible doesn't Paul also command wives to respect their husbands?

Without having a hermeneutically nuanced worldview, my daughters still had enough common sense as children to know that was silly. They didn't need to know the specific Bible reference to understand that poisoning others with addiction for profit was contrary to the character of God. Therefore, Mom shouldn't follow no matter how much Dad is breaking bad.

That acknowledges there is a chain of command. In other words, I might be the authority in the home as the husband/father, but I am not the highest authority—God is. And should I choose as their earthly father to no longer obey God, they should reject me and still obey their heavenly Father instead.

The same applies to government. Whenever government demands something of us that God says not to do or that belongs to Him, we are to obey God instead of government.

Or, as Christ put it, "Render unto Caesar that which is Caesar's, but render unto God that which is God's." Paul lived out this teaching, to the point it cost him his own life.

> Romans 13:1–7 is a civic application of universal Biblical truth asserted throughout the Bible: Christians are to obey God and not man.

Paul closes the passage in question with his own spin on "render unto Caesar" when he says, "Respect to whom respect is owed, honor to whom honor is owed." Nero asked something of Paul that Nero wasn't owed, namely to be obeyed as God or above God. In other words, Nero asked something of Paul that he *couldn't*, not merely *wouldn't*, give. Paul did not have permission to worship another god, to obey a false idol, or to deny Christ. His life was no longer his own, so Paul had no choice but to obey God instead of man, even the most powerful man in the world. Nero could destroy Paul's body, but God could cast his eternal soul into Hell. Paul was to follow the way, not the world.

Furthermore, Nero also didn't have permission to ask such a thing of Paul. Nero, despite being an uncircumcised pagan Caesar of Rome, was every bit as accountable to the one, true living God he didn't believe in as was the everyman known as Paul who did believe. God is God and there is no other, over all peoples, at all times, and in all places. You may reject gravity, but that doesn't mean you can fly. Gravity exists whether or not you acknowledge it. Likewise, God, the author of gravity, is God whether or not you worship Him.

> The primary purpose of human government is to punish evil in order to protect the righteous.

Paul writes that government is "a servant of God," thus making it an "avenger who carries out God's wrath on the wrongdoer." This is why Paul also says to obey the civil law, because when it is lawful it is based on divine revelation and performing a divinely ordained task. However, as Paul demonstrated with his own life, when the civil law denies its divine origin/jurisdiction then we are to follow the Word of God nevertheless. You see this quandary executed in one of the opening scenes of *Man of Steel*, when General Zod launches an angry insurrection against the Kryptonian government.

Zod attempts to enlist the assistance of his long-time friend and respected government critic, Jor-El. However, when Jor-El sees that Zod is embarking on a form of savagery that also violates the higher law that was supposed to be guiding the people, Jor-El declines to join with Zod and says, "I will honor the man you once were, Zod, and not this monster you've become." In other words, Jor-El refused to join with Zod for the same reason Jor-El himself was defying the Kryptonian government—both Zod and the government were violating the higher law.

God takes this divinely ordained role of human government so seriously that He also permits it to punish His people. Thus, the principle here cuts both ways. Just as we are to disobey earthly governments when they disobey God's law, earthly governments (even pagan ones) are permitted to punish believers when they disobey God in certain ways, too. We call them crimes. If as a believer I have too much to drink and then tragically take the life of another while inebriated behind the wheel of my car, God permits even a godless government to convict me of vehicular homicide.

So if Nero had lawfully convicted Paul of committing murder in his anger, Nero would've been within his divine right to execute Paul for such a crime even though Nero himself was a heathen. Similarly, a US president who heinously supports abortion of innocent babies is still right to execute adult serial killers. Because the character of God doesn't rest as much on the fallibility of man as it does the perfect justice of His law.

> Government is every bit as accountable to God as the governed.

Since it is instituted by God, appointed by God, and permitted by God, government is accountable to God. The same sinfulness that tempts us as citizens also tempts those citizens who reside within government. They are not more special than us. They are not our betters. If anything, the added temptation of that proximity to power and other people's money makes those within government even more prone to temptation. Our Founders understood this, which is why they viewed government to be both vital and limited. George Washington famously compared it to a fire. Both are a useful tool, but one that must be tended to regularly and kept from raging out of control.

> In our country, "we the people" formed the union and the Constitution that governs us. Our politicians are therefore public servants who only govern by our consent. So we are not to submit to them—they are to submit to us. Therefore, in the case of these United States, "we the people" are the instituted authority that God has appointed/permitted.

This means almost every sermon you've ever heard about this Bible passage, if you're even fortunate enough to attend a church that preaches a challenging book such as Romans, is too often turned on its head and addressed from the wrong premise. It is usually preached from the perspective of a people subservient to government, as opposed to our actual American tradition that government is subservient to the people. Policemen and soldiers are not granted the right to keep and bear arms in the Constitution, but the average American citizen is. And that is to explicitly codify who the real authority is here in these United States—"we the people."

As a Roman citizen, Paul was granted proto versions of the civil liberties we take for granted today. One of them was a right to habeas corpus, which Paul called upon as he was being stretched out to be flogged and perhaps executed. In other words, Paul did not deny his Roman citizenship but instead used it as a means to advance his apostolic mission. Likewise, if Paul was able to conform his Roman citizenship within his Christ-centered paradigm, we are free to do the same. Except our citizenship grants us authority over government via a representative framework, which is exactly what "government by the consent of the governed" in the Declaration of Independence means.

All the ultimate accountability in our system of government resides with the people. We vote them in and out of office and can even recall them before their terms are up in some cases. Just because we have currently abrogated our authority as "we the people" and allowed ourselves to be treated as plebians doesn't mean we truly are. Hence, if government is consistently failing the people in our country, it's because the people of this country are consistently failing themselves.

> As we enter into America's first post-Christian generation, every believer now needs to be prepared to tell its government "no." They must refuse to stand down on defining right versus wrong just to appease evolving cultural customs or authoritarian decrees—just as Paul did.

Some of you may be unsure if you could really tell the government (or authoritarian corporations for that matter) "No, there's really no such a thing as fifty-seven genders." Or could you refuse to attend mandatory critical race (racist) theory training when/if your time comes?

Well, I bring you glad tidings of great joy to close out this chapter. If you, as a believer, are unsure whether or not you have the courage of conviction to refuse to have your conscience violated, you are most definitely going to find out. In this post-Christian America we now live in, you will either comply or you will be made to care. Tolerance Boulevard is always a one-way street, and neutrality is futile.

Thus, as God said to Job, "gird up your loins" and be prepared for spiritual battle. Because I promise you, the fight is coming your way.

Group Discussion Questions:

1. Why do you think there's such confusion about Romans 13:1–7? Are compliance and subservience genuine Christian virtues in other parts of the Bible and only misapplied to rogue government? Are people simply looking for an excuse to explain away their cowardice or apathy? Or do you disagree with Steve's fundamental point? If so, why?

2. Name an issue or issues where present-day Caesars have usurped that which belongs to God. How have you (or would you have) intervened? How did the government respond? How did you respond (or would you respond) to the government's response?

3. If people no longer believe the primary purpose of government is to punish evil, what do they believe its primary purpose now is? How did that transition come to pass? Who is responsible?

4. How are the "we the people" of today most different from the "we the people" of our nation's founding, and is that a difference that fundamentally impacts the ability of the nation to continue thriving or even existing?

5. What example from history or even fiction can you regularly consult for inspiration when it comes to saying "no"?

Chapter 2

THE DECLARATION OF INDEPENDENCE

A prophet of old once said, "My people perish for lack of knowledge." Today our stunning lack of knowledge of what it is America really was founded to stand for puts us at risk to be the generation that sees liberty perish here.

Our Founding Fathers intended this holiday to be about much more than barbeques and camping trips. They intended it to be a commemoration of American Exceptionalism, which they then hoped would inspire others across the globe to seek self-governance and liberty in their own countries. Consider this excerpt from a letter Founding Father John Adams sent to his wife Abigail on July 3, 1776:[1]

> [Independence Day] will be the most memorable epoch in the history of America. I am apt to believe that it will be celebrated by succeeding generations as the great anniversary festival.

---

1   "Letter from John Adams to Abigail Adams, 3 July 1776, 'Had a Declaration...,'" *Adams Family Papers: An Electronic Archive*, Massachusetts Historical Society, https://www.masshist.org/digitaladams/archive/doc?id=L-17760703jasecond.

It ought to be commemorated, as the Day of Deliverance by solemn Acts of Devotion to God Almighty. It ought to be solemnized with pomp and parade, with shows, games, sports, guns, bells, bonfires and illuminations from one end of this continent to the other. From this time forward forever more. You will think me transported with enthusiasm but I am not. I am well aware of the toil and blood and treasure, that it will cost us to maintain this Declaration, and support and defend these States. Yet through all the gloom I can see the rays of ravishing light and glory. I can see that the end is more than worth all the means. And that Posterity will triumph in that days' transaction, even though we should rue it, which I trust in God we shall not.

Nowadays if you're a community that attempts to take John Adams's advice and put it into practice, you end up in court for violating the so-called separation of church and state (which appears precisely nowhere in the Constitution, by the way). Why have we strayed so far from the path to freedom our forefathers blazed for us?

I believe it's because most of us have never truly read, studied, and thus understood the words in our founding document—the Declaration of Independence.

In my opinion the Declaration is one of the greatest treatises ever written, and maybe the most powerful document composed without the benefit of direct divine inspiration in all of Western civilization. Given what was at stake, and the history that was riding on its every syllable, it had to be.

It's formatted like a legal argument, which is exactly what it was. There is the opening argument, which lays the groundwork for the case, followed by the presenting of evidence that reinforces the case, and then it concludes with the closing argument with the verdict to be rendered by history. Thematically it contains the essence of law, as in it was meant to be both binding and moral.

Much of its terminology and ideas are sadly foreign concepts to those of us worked over by political correctness, wokeness, and paganism (but I repeat myself), but they remain every bit as true and inspiring now as they were when the ink first fell from the pen of Thomas Jefferson. In this chapter we're going to look at each section of this magnum opus individually. Let us begin:

> *When in the Course of human events, it becomes necessary for one people to dissolve the political bands which have connected them with another, and to assume among the powers of the earth, the separate and equal station to which the Laws of Nature and of Nature's God entitle them, a decent respect to the opinions of mankind requires that they should declare the causes which impel them to the separation. We hold these truths to be self-evident, that all men are created equal, that they are endowed by their Creator with certain unalienable Rights, that among these are Life, Liberty and the pursuit of Happiness.—That to secure these rights, Governments are instituted among Men, deriving their just powers from the consent of the governed.—That whenever any Form of Government becomes destructive of these ends, it is the Right of the People to alter or to abolish it, and to institute new Government, laying its foundation on such principles and*

organizing its powers in such form, as to them shall seem most likely to effect their Safety and Happiness. Prudence, indeed, will dictate that Governments long established should not be changed for light and transient causes; and accordingly all experience hath shewn, that mankind are more disposed to suffer, while evils are sufferable, than to right themselves by abolishing the forms to which they are accustomed. But when a long train of abuses and usurpations, pursuing invariably the same Object evinces a design to reduce them under absolute Despotism, it is their right, it is their duty, to throw off such Government, and to provide new Guards for their future security. Such has been the patient sufferance of these Colonies; and such is now the necessity which constrains them to alter their former Systems of Government.

Right away Jefferson is letting you know this is a document of separation, or secession. These United States are seceding from the British crown. This is a divorce decree. And Jefferson also states the grounds for the divorce: the king of England has violated the highest law and done so repeatedly—which Jefferson refers to as "the Laws of Nature and Nature's God." Otherwise known as the natural law.

Remember that almost all of the original thirteen colonies were either founded or settled by some vestige of the Christian church. And in some of these Christian traditions, particularly Anabaptist ones like the Quakers in Pennsylvania, it was considered a clear violation of Romans 13 to rebel against earthly authorities (which is why we discussed Romans 13 in the chapter preceding this one). Thus, they didn't even have agreement with one another on the right to declare independence, before even addressing the specific case for it in their situation.

Jefferson attempts to transcend this debate among the colonists by appealing to something more transcendent. In doing so, Jefferson effectively authors the mission statement for American Exceptionalism: "We hold these truths to be self-evident, that all men are created equal, that they are endowed by their Creator with certain unalienable Rights. That among these are Life, Liberty, and the Pursuit of Happiness. That to secure these rights, Governments are instituted among Men, deriving their just powers from the consent of the governed."

In other words, there is a God and it's not government. And we know who they thought that God was, because in 1781 the Continental Congress authorized the printing of the "Aitken Bible" to make sure the British couldn't embargo English-speaking Bibles from these new United States.[2] That's the one and only time the US government officially endorsed a religious text, and it was the Bible. It's why we still take our oaths on it to this very day.

The Declaration also declares our rights come from the God of the Bible and not government. Therefore, government's only duty is the protection and preservation of those God-given rights, and a people doesn't have to consent to being governed by a government that is derelict in that God-given duty.

From there, Jefferson then enters into evidence twenty-seven grievances, or what he calls "repeated injuries and usurpations." This is a list of documented

---

2   Alyssa Roat, "What Was the First Bible Printed in America?" Christianity. com, July 9, 2020, https://www.christianity.com/wiki/bible/what-was-the-first-bible-printed-in-america.html.

injustices committed by King George III, which are in violation of not just good government but also the "Laws of Nature and Nature's God." Jefferson is now itemizing the case for divorce:

> The history of the present King of Great Britain is a history of repeated injuries and usurpations, all having in direct object the establishment of an absolute Tyranny over these States. To prove this, let Facts be submitted to a candid world.

> He has refused his Assent to Laws, the most wholesome and necessary for the public good.

> He has forbidden his Governors to pass Laws of immediate and pressing importance, unless suspended in their operation till his Assent should be obtained; and when so suspended, he has utterly neglected to attend to them.

> He has refused to pass other Laws for the accommodation of large districts of people, unless those people would relinquish the right of Representation in the Legislature, a right inestimable to them and formidable to tyrants only.

> He has called together legislative bodies at places unusual, uncomfortable, and distant from the depository of their public Records, for the sole purpose of fatiguing them into compliance with his measures.

> He has dissolved Representative Houses repeatedly, for opposing with manly firmness his invasions on the rights of the people.

He has refused for a long time, after such dissolutions, to cause others to be elected; whereby the Legislative powers, incapable of Annihilation, have returned to the People at large for their exercise; the State remaining in the meantime exposed to all the dangers of invasion from without, and convulsions within.

He has endeavored to prevent the population of these States; for that purpose obstructing the Laws for Naturalization of Foreigners; refusing to pass others to encourage their migrations hither, and raising the conditions of new Appropriations of Lands.

He has obstructed the Administration of Justice, by refusing his Assent to Laws for establishing Judiciary powers.

He has made Judges dependent on his Will alone, for the tenure of their offices, and the amount and payment of their salaries.

He has erected a multitude of New Offices, and sent hither swarms of Officers to harass our people, and eat out their substance.

He has kept among us, in times of peace, Standing Armies without the Consent of our legislatures.

He has affected to render the Military independent of and superior to the Civil power.

He has combined with others to subject us to a jurisdiction foreign to our constitution, and unacknowledged by our laws; giving his Assent to their Acts of pretended Legislation:

For Quartering large bodies of armed troops among us:

For protecting them, by a mock Trial, from punishment for any Murders which they should commit on the Inhabitants of these States:

For cutting off our Trade with all parts of the world:

For imposing Taxes on us without our Consent:

For depriving us in many cases, of the benefits of Trial by Jury:

For transporting us beyond Seas to be tried for pretended offences

For abolishing the free System of English Laws in a neighboring Province, establishing therein an Arbitrary government, and enlarging its Boundaries so as to render it at once an example and fit instrument for introducing the same absolute rule into these Colonies:

For taking away our Charters, abolishing our most valuable Laws, and altering fundamentally the Forms of our Governments:

For suspending our own Legislatures, and declaring themselves invested with power to legislate for us in all cases whatsoever.

He has abdicated Government here, by declaring us out of his Protection and waging War against us.

He has plundered our seas, ravaged our Coasts, burnt our towns, and destroyed the lives of our people.

He is at this time transporting large Armies of foreign Mercenaries to complete the works of death, desolation and tyranny, already begun with circumstances of Cruelty & perfidy scarcely paralleled in the most barbarous ages, and totally unworthy the Head of a civilized nation.

He has constrained our fellow Citizens taken Captive on the high Seas to bear Arms against their Country, to become the executioners of their friends and Brethren, or to fall themselves by their Hands.

He has excited domestic insurrections amongst us, and has endeavored to bring on the inhabitants of our frontiers, the merciless Indian Savages, whose known rule of warfare, is an undistinguished destruction of all ages, sexes and conditions.

Worth noting is that abuse of the judiciary is the most-named violation, similar to how statists today use unelected judges to usurp the Constitution in our time. There truly is nothing new under the sun.

In his closing argument, Jefferson reveals this divorce decree is not being taken lightly, or cavalierly on a whim. But only as a last resort once the Crown made it clear it wouldn't waver from its tyranny:

In every stage of these Oppressions We have Petitioned for Redress in the most humble terms: Our repeated Petitions have been answered only by repeated injury. A Prince whose character is thus marked by every act which may define a Tyrant, is unfit to be the ruler of a free people. Nor have We been wanting in attentions to our British brethren. We have warned them from time to time of attempts by their legislature to extend an unwarrantable jurisdiction over us. We have reminded them of the circumstances of our emigration and settlement here. We have appealed to their native justice and magnanimity, and we have conjured them by the ties of our common kindred to disavow these usurpations, which, would inevitably interrupt our connections and correspondence. They too have been deaf to the voice of justice and of consanguinity. We must, therefore, acquiesce in the necessity, which denounces our Separation, and hold them, as we hold the rest of mankind, Enemies in War, in Peace Friends.

Finally, Jefferson concludes in a most intriguing way. He invites God to judge the motives of those committing to this revolution, to the point of providence not permitting it to be successful if they are weighed, measured, and found wanting:

*We, therefore, the Representatives of the united States of America, in General Congress, Assembled, **appealing to the Supreme Judge of the world for the rectitude of our intentions,** do, in the Name, and by Authority* *of the good People of these Colonies, solemnly publish and declare, That these United Colonies are, and of Right ought to be Free and Independent States; that they are Absolved from all Allegiance to the British Crown, and that all political connection between them and the State of Great Britain, is and ought to be totally dissolved; and that as Free and Independent States, they have full Power to levy War, conclude Peace, contract Alliances, establish Commerce, and to do all other Acts and Things which Independent States may of right do. And for the support of this Declaration, with a firm reliance on the protection of divine Providence, we mutually pledge to each other our Lives, our Fortunes and our sacred Honor.* **[emphasis added]**

The bolded portion is the key here. The fifty-six men who are about to sign this document are not only pledging to one another their lives, fortunes, and sacred honors (which many of them paid), but pledging something to God as well.

The word rectitude means "morally correct behavior or thinking." Jefferson and his fellow co-signers are openly declaring to their Creator they believe their motives for doing this are righteous, but that ultimately it's up to the "Supreme Judge of the world" to determine that. And His determination in their favor is the only hope they have to be successful against such overwhelming odds, which is what "a firm reliance on the protection of divine providence" means. In colonial times, the term "providence" was often used as a reference to the sovereign will of God.

What you just learned is that the founding document of this country asserts four fundamentals:

The assertion that God's law is the highest law and must be obeyed above all other man-made laws.

Our human rights come from God alone.

God alone is the judge of our individual actions as well as our history.

We cannot hope to prevail against tyranny in this world without the sovereign will of God.

So much for the notion we were founded as a secular utopia, I suppose. The Biblical hermeneutic proclaimed by the Declaration of Independence is so sound that if we simply replaced references to King George III with attempts to confront any sinfulness from ourselves or others it would still stand as orthodoxy.

That's because while the Declaration of Independence was not directly divinely inspired, it was indirectly so. A Biblical worldview had so permeated the culture of the colonies that it couldn't help but infuse even the political pronouncements of those who themselves had heterodoxic religious viewpoints or hadn't given their lives to Christ. That culture is what gave birth to the greatest force for good in this world since the establishment of the Christian church, and that is a culture whose ideals are worthy of conserving if you ask me. You know a tree by its fruit, and the majority of the fruit produced by the country inspired by this culture has been good.

"But what about slavery" some of you reading this will ask, or may be asked by scoffers. Shouldn't the evils of slavery permanently disqualify any claims of American Exceptionalism, as the Spirit of the Age claims nowadays?

Any attempts at whitewashing the heinous scourge of slavery from our national archives should receive pushback from Christians. After all, we serve the Lord who sets the captives free. Abolition and Emancipation were inspired by and succeeded out of our churches. For whom the Son sets free is free indeed.

However, it's just not as simple as those held captive to Spirit of the Age indoctrination claim it to be. History, and human nature, never is.

For starters, slavery was the singular issue that threatened to stop these free and independent states from ever uniting from the beginning.[3] In his original draft of the Declaration, Jefferson specifically mentions the slave trade as a "cruel war against human nature itself" that violates "its most sacred rights of life and liberty in the persons of a distant people" in the list of grievances against King George III.

Eleven of the thirteen colonies approved, with only Georgia and South Carolina objecting out of fear that acknowledging this precedent would ultimately lead to abolition. So right away, there was a sizeable contingent within the Founding Fathers who recognized slavery was a heinous contradiction of their own mission statement. For example, Founding Fathers such as Benjamin Franklin, Alexander Hamilton, Benjamin Rush, and John Jay were already publicly declared abolitionists at this time.

The Spirit of the Age will then often point to the fact the Constitution forbade abolishing slavery for twenty years. But what it fails to tell you is the first incremental law aimed at ending the slave trade was signed by now President Jefferson *on the very first day the Constitution permitted it*—January 1, 1808. And this was more than twenty years after the Northwest Ordinance prohibited

---

3   Jonathan W. Pidluzny, "Four Things Every American Should Know About the Declaration of Independence," *The American Mind*, Claremont Institute, July 4, 2019, https://americanmind.org/salvo/four-things-every-american-should-know-about-the-declaration-of-independence/?.

slavery's expansion into the new territories of Indiana, Michigan, Minnesota, Ohio, and Wisconsin.

This means efforts to right this historic wrong were already underway immediately after the founding of the country. It simply isn't an intellectually honest view to either trivialize the evil of slavery, for which fissures still exist that we're wresting with in our society today, nor expand its guilt to tarnish every single thing America has stood for—especially after more than 600,000 Americans died on the battlefield over it.

The latter isn't mere historic revisionism, but a cultural hijacking, which has sadly been successful. To the point even several of you who are reading this now as committed patriots learned some of the truths of this chapter for the first time. Proof that still people perish for a lack of knowledge.

Group Discussion Questions:

1. Had you ever read the entire text itself or heard the entire Declaration of Independence broken down this way before, prior to reading this chapter? Why or why not?

2. What about the people you know, or the average American on the street—how would they answer that question?

3. How aware were you of how contested the issue of slavery was from the dawn of the republic? Were you taught that since they were all racists they all owned slaves or supported it?

4. Are America's failures, such as slavery, rooted in systemic bias of systems or systemic sinfulness of human beings? How might the answer to this influence what you believe the solution needs to be?

5. True or False: the entire premise of liberty rests on the principle our rights come from God and not government. Why or why not?

Chapter 3
CHOOSE THIS DAY

Sooner or later, every culture comes to a crossroads.
Sooner or later, every great nation is required to acknowledge who really is in charge here on Earth. Sooner or later, every great civilization in the history of this planet stares into the moral and spiritual abyss and is confronted with the greatest question ever posed to the God of the Bible.

That question is found in the thirty-eighth verse of the eighteenth chapter of John's gospel, and a pagan Roman governor who, unbeknownst to him, was staring directly at God incarnate is the one who posed it. Looking only to satisfy the politics of the moment, and thus failing to grasp the bigger picture of the monumental cosmic drama being played out within his very own realm, Roman procurator Pontius Pilate asked Jesus Christ a very simple yet salient question.

"What is truth?"

Without the correct answer to that question, every culture in history has come to a crossroads that ends in a path of destruction. Even a loving, sovereign God who is slow to anger and quick to forgive will only allow us so many chances to recognize who is really running the show down here.

Despite our numerous successes and failures throughout history, the self-governing nation that is these United States of America has endured because it asserted at its inception a most profound yet simple premise for establishing human freedom. Our Founding Fathers, morally flawed but simultaneously brilliant, made the case that it is the Creator (God of the Bible)—not a court, not a king, not a president, not a congress, not a specific church, not a religion, not a philosophy, nor anything else predicated on human ingenuity alone—that endows every human being with the right to life, liberty, and the pursuit of happiness.

I believe they did this because at that time in history the most powerful person on the planet was King George III. And as the king of Britain, he was master and ruler just as most kings claimed to be—by asserting that their power to rule over the populace came from God (and that's when they weren't claiming to be a god themselves).

The Declaration of Independence was constructed in such a manner to confront this paradigm. That's why it included all the infractions the king of England had made upon the freedoms of the colonials. They were building a case by the preponderance of the evidence. In their minds, the preponderance of the evidence clearly demonstrated that either God didn't appoint King George III ruler over them or he was governing them in a fashion that was ungodly because he was infringing upon their rights to life, liberty, and the pursuit of happiness. And since those rights came from God and King George III was obstructing them, that provided our Founding Fathers the moral wherewithal to declare independence from the British crown.

The premise was perfect, even if the people implementing it weren't. Slavery was a sin that we're still paying for in our balkanized culture today. Yet, for every colossal miscarriage of justice like the Dred Scott decision, there was an Emancipation Proclamation. Our notion of a divinely inspired freedom included in it the very mechanisms needed to correct our fallen, sinful urge to dominate our fellow man. It reflected God's sense of justice, even if it took stiff-necked people longer than He would've liked to get the message.

Those mechanisms were there because the fifty-six men who signed that Declaration of Independence—in which they pledged their lives, their fortunes, and their sacred honor—understood the true nature of human nature. All of them had some semblance of a Biblical worldview, a Judeo-Christian value system. They were as diverse in their own way as we are today. Some were more fervent in their Christian faith than others. Some were fiery fundamentalists, others didn't wear it on their sleeves, and a few others weren't even convinced that God was still directly caring for His creation—which left the door open for human reason influenced by the Enlightenment.

Yet, because of their shared Biblical view of the world, they understood that human beings were not to be trusted when left to our own devices. They themselves were ironically asserting individual liberty while several of them still owned slaves, so I would imagine they were keenly aware of how wicked the human heart truly is.

These men understood the concept of sin and what it had done to the human race. They may have differed in what their solution for it was, but they all agreed it was humanity's main problem. To these men of the eighteenth century, there was no doubt humanity needed saving. It was just a matter of who was responsible for saving it.

Unlike what our contemporary deep thinkers assert, they didn't believe that human beings were inherently good. That's why they created the clumsy system of checks and balances we have today. They knew it wasn't the most perfect or efficient system they could muster. Churchill famously observed that "democracy is the worst form of government except for all the others," but the Founders knew it was the only way to give self-governance to the depraved human condition.

We would have majority rule, yes, but with safeguards put into place to protect the minority. We would have democracy, yes, but in the form of a republic to prevent mob rule. We would have a chief executive, yes, but the people would elect him and our version of parliament would have the right to oversight. We would have an independent judiciary, yes, but to avoid a black-robed oligarchy this was actually the branch originally given the least amount of power. They implemented tension as a tactic, as their check and balance against man's inhumanity to man.

There would be freedom of speech so everyone had a voice. There would also be freedom of assembly and the right to keep and bear arms, so that the government would be afraid of the people as opposed to the other way around. To avoid the bloody Catholic-Protestant conflicts that had haunted their ancestors in Europe, there would not be a state religion; but at the same time the state was to make no law impeding the free exercise thereof.

Our Founding Fathers didn't agree about everything, but it seems as if they did agree with Lord Acton's admonition that "absolute power corrupts absolutely." So they created a paradox: government would be necessary to maintain law and order among a sinful people, but it would be limited to protecting the God-given rights of the people because, by definition, those within government were sinful, too.

There was a fly in the ointment, however, a flaw in the matrix. What if there would come a time when the people no longer recognized their rights came from their Creator, or what if there would come a time when the people accepted multiple interpretations as to who the Creator is?

Remember that we were still almost a century away from Darwinism sweeping the globe at the time the Declaration of Independence and our Constitution were ratified. We were still almost a century away from the idea that human beings were sporadically evolved and without sin because they had sprung from random microbes of amino acids and combustible carbons over countless epochs. But a whole new cultural and political philosophy was birthed out of Darwinism, one that led to the people looking at self-governance very differently.

After all, was it really necessary to have limited government if people are inherently good and just need to be educated so as to make better choices? Was Darwinian evolution limited to just natural selection and the origin of species within natural habitats and ecosystems? Could it apply intellectually, culturally, politically, and morally as well?

Would that mean that people could now evolve through education and experience to the point that they were qualified to redefine morality and truth for the masses? Better yet, did our concept of the Creator, if there still was one, evolve alongside with us and did that Creator itself evolve alongside the human condition? If that's possible, is it also possible that right and wrong are now negotiable based upon the situation or the individual they're being applied to?

If the people lost their moral compass, it wouldn't take long before everyone did as he or she saw fit, nor would it take long for the people to take advantage of their self-governance to institutionalize all forms of depravity and apostasy. And the people would seek to do that for the same reason Adam and Eve covered their nether regions when they sinned and realized they were naked. The human heart is deceitful above all things, and it doesn't like to be confronted with the truth of its own deceitfulness.

So in America we have come to pass laws and elect leaders who can define what we want right and wrong to be according to popular whim. It's far less messy than what the ancient Israelites did when confronted with their sin—they usually murdered their prophets. In America we just self-appoint new ones that tickle our ears.

Speaking prophetically in 1798, Founding Father and second President of the United States John Adams addressed this potential danger of self-governance when he said the following:

> We have no government armed in power capable of contending with human passions unbridled by morality and religion. Our Constitution was made only for a religious and moral people. It is wholly inadequate for the government of any other.

Maybe that's why our Constitution is now considered a living, breathing document? In a nation as spiritually confused and Biblically illiterate as this one currently is, should it surprise us that most Americans believe the saying "the Lord helps those who help themselves" is found in the Bible and that the doctrine of "separation of church and state" is found in the Constitution? Neither is, by the way, in case you're scoring at home.

Thus, since politics is faith and ethics in action, it shouldn't be a surprise that when our faith is fleeting our politics are futile.

Which is why I believe this nation is being tested at this very moment like never before. As a culture we are staring into the abyss, as have other notable civilizations before us. We are again being asked who is really running the show. Whom do we really trust? Who really is God?

There is a choice before us as a people. There's the macro choice we must make collectively as a civilization, and then the micro choice we must each make as individuals. The scope is different, but the choice is the same.

If the Spirit of the Age is god, then worship it accordingly. But if God is God, then worship Him as He demands instead. Without apology and in full witness of a watching world.

As for you and your house, where do you stand?

Group Discussion Questions:

1. What is your understanding of the Declaration of Independence's reliance on truth as defined by "the laws of Nature and Nature's God"?

2. How is truth, in fact, self-evident? How can you explain that to both the ignorant and the enemy?

3. If all men are "created equal," what does that mean in theory and in practice? What doesn't that mean? How do you know?

4. How are rights, in fact, inalienable? How can you explain that to both the ignorant and the enemy? Why are life, liberty, and the pursuit of happiness fundamental to an American foundational understanding?

5. How must we sacrifice our lives, fortunes, and sacred honors going forward to preserve, protect, and defend our national inheritance from slipping away?

Chapter 4

THE INCONVENIENT TRUTH ABOUT AMERICA

This should not come from the likes of me.

I've only been a Christian since 2003. I've grown quite a bit in my faith, and I've been very public and bold about it on numerous public platforms. But I'm still a work in progress. I have blind spots. I have weak spots. I have red light districts in the brain. I've had problems in marriage. I've had problems in my personal life.

I'm not an apostle. I'm not a pastor. I'm not a prophet. I'm just a guy named Steve. Somebody who is a much more finished work should be delivering this message. It should come from somebody better than me. We've sat around waiting for that to happen, but unfortunately with a few exceptions messages like this have not. So we are left wandering in the desert.

Shortly before writing this I watched the documentary *The Rise of Jordan Peterson*. I was struck by the number of young men coming up to him after his talks, broken with tears in their eyes. Basically he was doing the job their dads should have been doing all along but hadn't. The job a pastor, a priest, a minister, a shepherd should have done but hadn't. His message is very powerful, and I want to emulate that in this chapter, except in a specifically Biblical context.

In the New Testament, the Apostle Paul writes a series of epistles, and in several of them he is addressing specific concerns about the community of believers in those specific situations. For example, in Galatia they had a particular problem with a group called Judaizers, so Paul specifically addresses that for the people and the church in that community. It doesn't mean there weren't broader themes there, which is why we are still sharing catechesis based on Paul's letters 2,000 years later, but the inspiration for them was a specific situation.

Of course, I'm not worthy to strap the Apostle Paul's sandals, but I'm going to do my best to emulate his process. Specifically, what are the issues we as American believers are facing? Are we sons of Issachar? As in do we understand the times and what to do about them?

Christ called to us to read and study and know the signs of the times. A lack of discernment is not permitted for the believer. The world is supposed to come to us for that. After all, we've got the owner's manual to the universe: the Word.

So I think it is time for us to come now and reason together. We need to face the inconvenient truth about America. It is time for some brutal honesty about where we are and where we are headed. We need a new black-robed regiment to help us discern this culture and the time we are in.

Right now, sadly, there isn't much of one. Sure, we have pockets of it, which is better than nothing, but we don't really have a unified black-robed regiment. So I'm going to do my best as one guy with one book to fill that void. These are some inconvenient truths we need to confront, acknowledge, and absorb.

One: We must see ourselves more as pilgrims now than patriots. The America we have been attempting to conserve is gone. The fundamentals of our culture and heritage are gone. We need to let go of our nostalgia. It is paralyzing us. Now tradition and nostalgia are not the same thing. Tradition is how we look back in the past and see how things work, and understand that if we update them for the times we are in they will work again in the future. While the process may need updating, the principle still works.

But nostalgia causes us to want to re-create the process instead, and the principle gets lost. We get myopic when we think it has to look just like (fill in the blank) because this is how it looked before. We get hooked on nostalgia. I believe right now we are paralyzed by nostalgia. We have to let go of nostalgia for America and embrace the mission we have as pilgrims living in America.

The good news is we didn't have to risk life and limb on a rickety boat where many of us died, and after we landed in North America we didn't have to watch half of us die the first two winters due to disease and starvation. But aside from those calamities, in every other definition of the word we are pilgrims in this era now. In many of the places we are going to go, what we believe is either anathema or new.

Two: We must also see ourselves more as Sons of Liberty than Founding Fathers. The times we are living in call back much more to a 1776 than to a 1789. We are no longer in control of the institutions that collectively guide our society, but we are now countercultural insurgents seeking to defy authoritarian attempts to impose the Spirit of the Age's will via coercion and corruption.

The Sons of Liberty lived in a pre-Constitution world. They hadn't even conceived that document yet. We now live in a post-Constitution world. Again, we are not conserving something. We are restarting it.

Three: America was founded as a Judeo-Christian country with limited government, but we are now a pagan country with limited liberty. Unless we accept this truth, we have no chance to survive let alone succeed, for we are deceiving ourselves regarding the scope of the challenge. You cannot defeat an enemy you don't acknowledge or know, nor can you solve a problem you don't acknowledge or know. There is no silent majority anymore. It doesn't exist. Furthermore, our belief system is in danger of being silenced in this society.

Four: The Constitution is effectively a dead letter. The natural law it codifies of course remains as it always has and always will because it is the code of the Creator, but its parameters and principles are effectively null and void. Even when the Constitution is defended by our politicians and judges it is usually on a technicality, not its original premise. Remember when the Republicans opposed Obamacare for a decade on the grounds "we couldn't afford it" rather than the grounds it is not even unconstitutional but anti-Constitutional? As in the purpose of the legislation was to undo the scheme of the Constitution itself.

So if we could afford anti-Constitutional legislation then it is good? It was a terrible argument, which shows you they didn't really mean it because when you gave them the power to do something about it after fifty show votes to repeal it "root and branch," they never did.

Think of poor Jack Phillips, apparently the only cake baker in all of Denver, Colorado. They keep spiritually assaulting that guy, demanding he has to use his business in order to promote their pagan mythology. He keeps refusing. The last time he won at the Supreme Court the

Court told the State of Colorado if they could come up with a different rationale than religious animus it was totally cool. Just don't make it about something icky we can't defend.

That's not defending the Constitution. That's not upholding it. That's unravelling it, Weezer style, as in the *Sweater Song*, just one thread at a time. As opposed to the Spirit of the Age, which is outright lighting it on fire whole cloth. Only the rate of unraveling is in dispute.

Five: We have wasted decades in the Republican Party on a national level with no real fruit to show for it whatsoever. Even within the one area where we had seen progress—Second Amendment rights—we are retreating now. The last two former presidents, including the Republican one, both issued unconstitutional gun control executive orders. The Second Amendment is in the Constitution. The words "executive order" strangely are not. The NRA's leadership is in shambles at the moment, and that was our most effective issue advocacy organization of the last couple of decades.

Six: We need to let go of the nostalgia of Americana's symbols and institutions. West Point announced critical racist theory was going to be part of its curriculum. You read that right—West Point. These institutions are all gone now. And they aren't just gone. They are against. They have been turned against us.

The time is coming soon when we may be the ones who refuse to stand for the red, white, and blue pomp and circumstances, which is really now just woke agitprop. We need to let go of that. The nostalgia is going to paralyze us. It is paralyzing us now. It is stopping us from seeing the truth of the situation we are in.

Seven: We need to at least consider we will no longer have free and fair elections like we took for granted for so long, and therefore we need to consider some alternative means for acting on our beliefs and defending ourselves. And then even if we continue to have free and fair elections, we are not going to merely vote our way out of this.

First of all, who are we actually going to vote for in most of these cases even if the vote and the election are secure and sound? It's not like Team GOP is flying those bold colors these days.

Now, thankfully if you are a Christian, you have a place called America because a large cloud of witnesses that preceded you for 2,000 years figured out how to advance their beliefs and values without anyone even knowing what voting was. We are going to have to recover some of those means. Get reacquainted with terms like "civil disobedience" because the war is coming to your front door. And you will not be permitted to abstain.

You will not be permitted to say, "I'll tell you the truth of what's happening if you leave my name out of this; I can't risk the smoke." History shows those who say "leave my name out of this" today out of fear of the mob will be the ones hauled away by the mob tomorrow.

Eight: We will imminently be banned from any and all mainstream platforms of significance in this country. That could mean tomorrow. That could mean five years from now. But we are on borrowed time. It's almost as if Gutenberg invented the printing press, Luther figured out he could use the new development to get his message out, and then Gutenberg decided to sell out to the Spirit of the Age and get woke and refuse to print any more of that Jesus stuff.

That's what social media has done. It's our new city gate where the vast majority of information is disclosed and distributed in our culture today, but it is with increasing rapidness refusing to give contrarian views distribution. We are all going to be gone unless these big tech communities are broken up for being the monopolies they are. All of us. Imminently. Unless we see some politicians grow a spine for a change and go after big tech on antitrust grounds.

Nine: We need to create our own subculture and ecosystem, not with a monastic intent of living separately but with the missional intent of modeling righteousness and liberty to a watching world. This means forming not a separate culture but an alternative one. A city within a city, if you will. Where our marriages are better. Our families are better. A better way of life. A superior way to live that prompts other people to say, "Wow, I want what they have." We run our businesses better. We run our schools better. This needs to be our priority. We need to create our own subculture and ecosystem, and if we don't do that, we will fail our children and grandchildren and their generation will succumb to the Spirit of the Age.

Ten: There are not enough of us to completely overtake the Spirit of the Age, I'm afraid. Too many Americans just want to be ruled. After a generation of indoctrination and being prepped for it, they seek out subservience. However, at the same time there are too many of us for the Spirit of the Age to assert itself completely, so we have a sort of standoff right now. We must establish a foothold while this standoff exists. We must make red states and red counties and red communities red again, and they must be at least as red as California is blue. We must take advantage of the balkanization to congregate in places where we strengthen the existing majority's foothold to withstand assaults from the Spirit of the Age. Because soon the standoff will end now that they own all the institutions, and it will be the Spirit of the Age on the prowl seeking whom it may devour. Take advantage of the time that is left and establish safe havens where the doctrine of the lesser magistrate reigns and where a militant form of federalism will be practiced. Create no-go zones for the Spirit of the Age, where it wouldn't even dare to attempt to impose its will on us for fear of the backlash.

Eleven: When we work inside structures within the broader culture—our jobs, a political party (likely the Republican Party), whatever the case may be—we must see ourselves as subversives, not just servants. If I'm running for office as a Republican, I don't give a wit about the Republican Party as a whole. I only care about what it does for me and how I can use it. I don't let it use me. I'm not an agent of it. I'm using it. I'm the subversive here.

Same with your job. Why do you think you have those talents and skills? So you could show up to the board meeting that day they announced critical racist theory is your new human resources protocol, and God merely put you there to shut up about the evil you are now going to be using those talents and gifts for? Nope.

Now that doesn't mean, by the way, we are just eager to be martyred. In the gospels Christ said right then was not the time for a direct confrontation, or proclamation of His lordship, several times. He didn't go traipsing around Galilee with a Messiah shirt on everywhere He went.

But when the time came, when the time was right, and the high priest looked at Him and said, "Are you the one? Enough, let's cut to the chase. Are you the Messiah?" That's when Christ looked boldly at him in front of all those who put Him on trial and quoted from the Prophet Daniel: "You will see the Son of Man coming on the clouds of Heaven."

He let them know. He laid down ordinance. He told them what's up. When the time was right, He announced Himself and with gusto. There will be a time that is right for all of us to do the same. Until then, be quietly subversive, but not weakly.

56

You are afraid of losing your job. You are afraid of blowback. That's not why you are there. You are there so that when the time is right, your Creator will pull from His quiver the arrow with your name on it and fire you across the bow of the Spirit of the Age. That is really why you are there.

We have no real allies beyond those with whom we share priorities and principles in common. Do not set yourself up therefore for betrayal and ambush. You are a stranger in a strange land almost everywhere you go now. But remember this: the Kingdom of God forcefully advances, and it is forceful men who lay hold of it. Not passive ones. Forceful ones.

Finally, all these previous eleven points are really holding actions. Because this is the bottom line: revival or bust. If there is not another Great Awakening here, the likes of which gave birth to liberty on this continent in the first place, liberty will be lost on this continent. Period. End of sentence. Collectively, without revival, these previous eleven realizations/steps will fail. But even if that unfortunately happens, we'll go down swinging as a civilization and maybe even see the Lord add some more of our countrymen to the eternal Kingdom that really matters.

Now, again, I'm the last person who should be issuing marching orders to God's people. Somebody better than me should be telling you these things. Somebody who has been more righteous or holy in their lives should be telling you these things. Somebody who wants less vengeance on his enemies than I do, and carries less spite around than I do every day. The anger just grows inside me every day about what goes on in our country. I have to resist the temptation to not just lose my mind on social media every day. I am so angry some days. Plenty of times I want to march down into the Valley of Elah and slay the uncircumcised Philistine who dares blaspheme the living God.

Somebody who doesn't wrestle with those things, who is better at showing the joy of the Lord, should have told you this. But we don't have any more time left to wait around for the people who have those characteristics to equip us for the times in which we are in. The hour is late. So I guess that leaves it to unfinished products like me. I hope that this was helpful.

Group Discussion Questions:

1. Are there already examples of times you have been either subversive or confrontational toward the Spirit of the Age in your workplace or public settings? Are there examples of times you regret not having done so? If so, why didn't you?

2. Is nostalgia one of the most common forms of idolatry facing American Christians? Do you have examples in your own life of giving undue or misplaced respect to things that are only due to God?

3. Do you agree that we are now living in a pagan, post-Christian country? If not, why? If so, how should your witness change, if at all? What are likely to be the most significant and persistent challenges for a Christian living under pagan rule?

4. Be brutally honest: What are your most significant pagan/ secular/nostalgic addictions that make living a compelling Christian witness the most difficult?

5. What quality of a pilgrim or Son of Liberty do you feel you must reclaim as an individual, or the nation must reclaim as a whole, in order to make a positive impact in the culture?

Chapter 5
THE PARABLE OF THE PARACHUTE

L et me use this chapter to tell you a story.

There once was a man piloting a plane that was about to crash. Against the advice of the air traffic controllers, those that shepherd the skies if you will, the man had decided he could pilot his plane through a storm and save fuel and time because it was the most direct route to his destination.

He took the easy way. He took a shortcut. He took matters into his own hands.

Sure, there were those who had warned him against flying through the storm. They were by and large more experienced flyers than he was, so they might have known what they were talking about but they had no idea he was in a hurry. He had somewhere he had to be, and he couldn't be late.

Plus, fuel those days wasn't cheap, and he was on a tight budget. He might've been able to afford the fuel costs of going the safer way, but then once he arrived at his destination he would lack the resources necessary to have the fun he was planning on having once he got there. *Who are these air traffic controllers anyway?* he thought. *Who died and made them boss?*

He had flown in poor weather before and dodged lightning strikes and turbulence each and every time. He didn't need to learn from the mistakes of others. He knew what he was doing. After all, those that can't do, teach. Right?

Unfortunately, now after failing to have his mayday heard because of radio interference from the storm, and with the sad reality confronting him that he had tempted fate recklessly once too often, he still wasn't willing to swallow his pride.

He refused to believe his fait accompli was about to be accomplished. He refused to accept that he couldn't keep his plane airborne. He still believed if it was meant to be then it's up to me.

Then, suddenly, out of the corner of his eye he saw a parachute. It had been gathering mothballs for ages, and he wasn't even sure he remembered how to strap it on and use it. He had always prided himself on never having to abandon ship and his—up until now anyway—perfect flying record.

For a moment all his pride was stripped away, and the conviction that his life was really at stake entered into his mind. His thoughts began to joust with one another.

One part of him said: "This is silly. Take the parachute. Eject. It's just a plane. It's not worth your life. You're being given a second chance to live here, make up for some things you wish you could do differently. You can choose life. This is a no-brainer. Count this is as a blessing and get rescued."

On the other hand, another part of him said: "Never give up. You can do it. You've made it this far when others doubted you. When the going gets tough, the tough get going. You're not going to surrender now, are you? You're not a weakling. You don't need that parachute to save you. Besides, does the parachute even work anyway? It's been there for so long that it might fail once you jump, and then you've traded one death for another that is even more macabre. At least this way you control your own fate. If you jump, it's all up to the parachute. But if you stay and fight, you've got a fighting chance to live."

Now, guess which side of the man's brain won out?

The man decided the parachute was too risky, and he wasn't going to rely on something else to rescue him. He knew the way to keep the plane airborne, he knew the truth of how to fly all on his own, and he knew this was his best shot to keep his life.

Or so he thought.

He thought wrong.

Hours later, when investigators combed through the wreckage of the man's plane and needed dental records to identify his gruesome remains, the one thing they found intact was the parachute.

One of the investigators said to the other, "Wasn't this man told how he could be saved? Wasn't he trained on how to use the parachute?"

Soberly, the other investigator pointed out that he must have been trained on how to be saved via the parachute because it's required in order to get a pilot's license. However, there are those who refuse to believe they need rescuing under any circumstances and just pay lip service to the training as a means to an end. And then they sadly crash and burn because in their minds it's about being in control, being brave, and being on the edge. They never consider the fact they're dead because they violated the law of gravity.

Even though they ignore the law of gravity, or act as if they alone have what it takes to defy it, the law of gravity is always there. It never changes. He's not the first pilot to play games with the law of gravity when he could've just chosen the parachute and lived. And he sadly won't be the last.

Later, after a period of mourning and the funeral, grief turned to bitterness, anger, and resentment for the dead pilot's family.

Yet ironically, the dead pilot's family hardly knew him. He spent more time at work than he did at home. He was more intimate with his secretary than he was his own wife. He knew more about his favorite sports teams than he did about his own children. Still, he was the only father and husband they knew, and they struggled to find meaning in this tragedy. The family needed somebody to blame, so they sued the local company that made the parachute.

They thought, *Clearly the parachute had to be defective? Or maybe he wasn't aware there even was a parachute, and that's why it wasn't used and there wasn't enough information out there that this parachute could save his life.*

It never occurred to them that the man had consciously chosen of his own free will not to use the parachute.

With the CEO of the local parachute company away tending to other business, the board of directors was left to deal with this lawsuit and public relations disaster on their own. Or at least that's what most of them thought. However, before he left the CEO had gone over his instructions to them very carefully, anticipating situations just like this might occur while he was away.

Yet the CEO had been gone for so long that most of the board ignored him, had completely forgotten what he told them, or doubted that he was ever going to return at all to hold them accountable.

This faction split into two groups.

On one side were those who believed the family had hired an ambulance chaser and were just trying to cash in on the death of the pilot. Some of these folks had actually hung out with the pilot before he died and were well aware of what he was up to behind closed doors in his private life when his family wasn't around.

They never confronted the pilot about not using the parachute, either. "Stupid is as a stupid does," or so they thought. "The dead pilot got exactly what he deserved, didn't he? He paid the stupid tax for not using the parachute, and when he crashed and burned that was payment in full, no questions asked."

They dared the family to take them to court and figured a pool of jurors from a community that was tired of the lack of personal responsibility these days would see it their way as well. To them it was all about the bottom line; they never assumed the family was really hurting and acting out like this as a result.

On the other side were those members of the board who sympathized greatly with the family, and they recognized the harshness of those on the board who didn't. They thought the company should generously settle out of court, even though the man was aware of the parachute before he took flight.

When the board voted against doing this, they decided it was time to start their own company; one that wouldn't be so focused on holding pilots accountable to the law of gravity, but rather to the benefits of the parachute. "In fact," they rationalized, "maybe they didn't need to call it a parachute any more at all?"

Calling these safety devices parachutes might lead folks to think their new company was just like the old one, and they were ashamed of the way their old company treated the family and suspected that many others in the community were as well.

So they decided to create a new safety device they reasoned could have all the benefits of the parachute, but one people felt better about using. They decided to tell people their new safety device was simply for softer landings, never bothering to inform them about the law of gravity. On top of that, they also didn't aggressively advertise their new safety device to the community, either.

They were concerned that through marketing the product they might make claims about the safety device that couldn't be backed up, and they weren't even sure that their safety device was any better or different than what any other company made. In their minds the important thing was that every pilot had access to some sort of safety device; it didn't matter which one or even the best one.

However, beyond these two factions within the parachute company's board of directors was a small remnant of those who remained faithful to the original vision of their CEO.

They grieved for the death of the pilot along with his family's loss, regardless of his peccadilloes, and made attempts to care for the loved ones who blamed the crash on them in the first place. Yet they also understood that the law of gravity is there for a reason and the pilot was responsible for obeying it. So while they awaited the CEO's return, they decided they needed to make a renewed effort to make sure that pilots realized the law of gravity was there, why it was there, what would happen if they didn't obey it, and why the parachute is provided in the first place.

The remnant that stayed with the company during this terrific ordeal remembered the words of the CEO. They put those wise words into practice, believing that's what the CEO would've done if he were here now and what he will do when he eventually returns. Their CEO had told them the law of gravity is good. It keeps everything grounded. However, since pilots can't help but try to escape the law of gravity—it's the very nature of their job to do so—they need a parachute to save them in the event they violate it.

In other words, the law of gravity is there for their protection, but the parachute is there to rescue them when they break the law. However, until pilots are first made aware of the law of gravity, they have no need for the parachute. And, of course, since the law of gravity applies to all of us, that means everyone has use for the parachute. Sounds like a win-win for everybody. Yet amazingly not everybody thinks so, and because of pride they continue to challenge the law of gravity to this very day without a parachute.

So far the law of gravity is undefeated.

Thank God for that parachute.

Group Discussion Questions:

1. For those with ears to hear, let them hear: What is the airplane? The parachute? The CEO? The board? Gravity?

2. Why does today's world so frequently reject the parachute? If gravity obviously isn't optional or particularly complicated but easy to reject nonetheless, what does that say about truth?

3. What changes can or should be made to the board so that it is more than just an easily ignored remnant of what it once was? Who has authority to make those changes?

4. Do some airplanes give pilots a false sense of security? Are they advertised as being too safe? Are our pilot schools doing a terrible job?

5. What are some plane crashes you've witnessed that not too long ago ythought to be impossible?

Chapter 6
BALANCE

The dictionary defines the word *balance* as "a state of equilibrium, to be equal and proportionate...mental steadiness and emotional stability, leading to habits of calm behavior, judgment, etc. The power or ability to decide an outcome by throwing one's weight, influence, or support to one side or the other. Equality between the totals on two sides of an account."

With that established as our plumbline, I sadly believe that THE CHURCH in America is all too often out of balance today. But just to make sure we are on target with this assessment, let's look at each of these definitions one by one.

A state of equilibrium, to be equal and proportionate.

Sunday mornings are still one of the most segregated times in America. Some ministries continue to add full-time staff, while others in the same community have their pastors working full-time jobs and then trying to shepherd the flock with whatever time is left. Some ministries spend millions building or remodeling new facilities on top of the ones they already have, while other ministries in the same community struggle to pay their bills and keep their doors open.

In the early church, "All the believers were together and had everything in common." And no, this isn't the Bible coming out for socialism, which is state-mandated wealth redistribution. Quite the contrary, when God set up a direct theocracy in Old Testament Israel, the system of taxation (or tithing) He installed wasn't even progressive in nature. All, rich and poor alike, paid the same 10 percent rate. Of course, 10 percent to the wealthy is more than to the downtrodden, but the Kingdom of God is a meritocracy not a socialist redistribution. To whom much is given much is required, yes, but whoever is faithful in a lot is given even more, while whoever is faithless in a little will even have that taken away.

There was no system to punitively punish success in God's economy as we try to do, which is why New Testament believers took it upon themselves to share among each other as a private community. The idea that a godless state would need to come in and demand they practice the love for one another Christ commanded was anathema. This was an automatic outpouring of the Holy Spirit at work in their lives. Can you say the same thing about THE CHURCH today? Are we sharing resources as a body of believers within an individual congregation this way, let alone a body of believers within a community? That's what I thought.

Mental steadiness and emotional stability, leading to habits of calm behavior, judgment, etc.

If we were living up to this, would our culture be in the condition it's currently in? Dudes who feel pretty are peeing in women's bathrooms for goodness sake.

The power or ability to decide an outcome by throwing one's weight, influence, or support to one side or the other.

America is home to some of the largest congregations in church history. Heck, several of those are located in the People's Republic of California, which is the epicenter for American paganism. Spiritually active and government-engaged Christians only make up 9 percent of the US population according to researcher George Barna, but they represented 14 percent of the overall electorate in the 2020 presidential election.[4] Over 70 percent of Americans claim to be Christian according to Pew Research.[5]

And yet, can we say by any objective measure that Judeo-Christian influence upon America is on the rise or even holding steady? Nope, quite the contrary, which is why we are living in the first post-Christian age in American history. The Bible says God's Word "does not return void" to Him, so if we have all these numbers and so little results to show for it, that is a huge "us" problem.

Equality between the totals on two sides of an account.

Now we're getting somewhere. I submit that this last definition is why we aren't meeting the previous three, either. THE CHURCH is out of balance at its core because the balance of grace and truth that defines its health and effectiveness is a mess.

That's a problem because it is the balance that Christ himself struck here on Earth. If Christ Himself was full of grace and truth, shouldn't it stand to reason that His church should be, too?

---

4   Tony Perkins, "Christian Conservatives Shatter Turnout Records for Trump," Family Research Council, December 2, 2020, https://www.frc.org/updatearticle/20201202/christian-conservatives.

5   "Religious Landscape Study," Pew Research Center, https://www.pewforum.org/religious-landscape-study/.

For perhaps the first time in American history, THE CHURCH finds itself corporately on the defensive in this culture. It's no longer *the* institution in town but just *an* institution, and many folks in the community not attending it believe that those who do should be committed to one. Many of the oldest churches in our cities are just historical landmarks in the midst of secularization, mere throwbacks to a bygone era. They have become a hidden city on the hill, and they're only discovered when someone needs to book a wedding.

For THE CHURCH to become vibrant, necessary, and relevant in people's lives again it doesn't need another food pantry, coffee bar, preaching limited to the King James Version, or dumbing down the Word. It needs to strike the balance of grace and truth.

There is no force in the universe more transformative than the grace of God.

The grace of God turned a murderer with a speech impediment into a deliverer and the ultimate lawgiver. The grace of God turned a teenage shepherd into the ultimate warrior and a great king. The grace of God turned a religious legalist who was a prideful persecutor into one of the most humble and effective spokesmen for God's love in the history of the planet. The grace of God turned a coward into the courageous Cephas, or rock. The grace of God took a baby born in a barn and turned Him into the King of Kings and Lord of Lords.

The grace of God transformed me, too.

I was born out of wedlock to a scared, dirt-poor fifteen-year-old girl living in what used to be called "the South Side bottoms" in Des Moines. Yet here I am decades later, broadcasting daily on one of the largest platforms in America. I tell you these things so that you recognize there's nothing special about me. There's no training I've been given to prepare me for where I am currently. There's no rational explanation for me doing what I am doing, saying what I am saying, and writing what I am writing. I have never applied for one of my broadcasting jobs, and I've never even sent in an audition tape to get any of those jobs, either. They've literally all been given to me without my doing anything. People I didn't previously know have always just called me out of the blue with opportunities I didn't previously know about.

The only answer that possibly explains how I ended up here from where I started is Christ. For whatever reason, He chose me as His workmanship to do good works, which were prepared in advance for me to do. Despite all my faults, shortcomings, and temptations (including the ones I still struggle not to give in to). One of those good works was encouraging all of you to go about enthusiastically and passionately doing what Christ has prepared for you as well, which is why I am writing this book.

The only reason for hope in my life has been Christ, and the only reason for hope in this world is Christ as well. He is my all in all. Without Him, I'm just a semi-professional video game player. Why did He save me and bless me? I don't know, because I certainly haven't done anything to deserve it.

That's why they call it grace.

Grace intimidates us because it reminds us of how inadequate we are on our own. Grace is agile, mobile, and hostile because grace transforms people and groups we've previously written off into world-changers. Grace gets us out of our comfort zones. Grace is God's undeserved favor poured out on humanity. But sadly, our rebellious, sinful nature leads us at times to resent the fact we can't earn it for ourselves no matter how clever, moral, rich, and accomplished we are. Because of our fallen nature we sometimes ironically end up running away from the very thing that saves us—grace.

Truth is our means to freedom. Without truth we don't know good from evil, and if we can't recognize the difference between the two, we can be led like lambs to slaughter—believing the things that destroy us are what's good for us or even fun. Without truth we don't know who God is and who we are. If we don't know who God is nor who we really are, we're lost, like the blind leading the blind. We lack meaning and purpose in our life. We're just marking time on the third rock from the sun.

Without truth we can't separate fact from fiction and wander aimlessly looking for the new hotness. That can be a talk show, a self-help guide, worldly philosophy, or a relationship. We become impetuous, needy, and desperate, and those emotional conditions greatly enhance the chances of making bad choices. The funny thing is, though, that by the world's standard the ability to engage in dangerous activities and behaviors, living only for today, and having an "open mind" to all forms of meaningless or destructive psychobabble are considered characteristics of freedom!

Yet that doesn't sound like freedom to me at all. Just wantonly doing things I know are bad for me, believing my life is entirely on my shoulders because I'm the only one I can count on in the end, not knowing why I was even born, and constantly changing whom or what I trust and believe in sound more like bondage. Actually, to put it more bluntly, it sounds like Hell.

Truth leads to faith, and faith comes only by the hearing of the Word. It's impossible to please God without faith, so we better know the truth in order to receive God's grace. Too much grace for the sake of truth makes us lazy, lenient, and lackadaisical. Too much truth for the sake of grace makes us cold, callous, and condemning.

Jesus says, "I am the way, the *truth*, and the life." Jesus also says, "It is the *truth* that shall set you free, and whom the Son sets free is free, indeed." Furthermore, Jesus declares, "For this reason I came into the world, to testify to the truth."

See, contrary to what you may have heard, Jesus isn't just some happy-go-lucky hippie of antiquity tiptoeing through the effervescent fields of Galilee with His band of merry men, sipping an espresso while pondering the lint in His navel and quoting Jack Kerouac. He's making an exclusive claim on truth. He's not only saying He knows it but that He *is* it.

On the other hand, Christ also isn't some harsh taskmaster who's waiting to pounce on us at any moment after making His list and checking it twice. In fact, in one parable Jesus says this about those who look at Him this way: "Throw that worthless servant outside, into the darkness, where there will be weeping and gnashing of teeth."

Jesus isn't mad because the servant failed, but because the servant assumed He would be mad at him if he screwed up—and that fear paralyzed him into doing nothing with the gifts he was given. Christ's perfect love casts out all fear, but the servant's lack of faith in who his master truly was led him to reject his master's grace.

God is not interested in what you can do for Him. He's far more interested in what He's done for you and then what He can do through you for others. That's the truth of the power of God's grace in our lives.

God's grace says get beyond your traditions, formalities, rules, rituals, and stained-glass windows and get your hands dirty with engagement, even if that means modernizing your approach somewhat for the modern age. God's truth also says you can modernize all you want, have all the coffee and donuts between services you want, and even have a slammin' praise team, but if you aren't making disciples with the Word made flesh when you do these things then you're just people taking up space.

So are you team grace or team truth? The answer better be yes.

Group Discussion Questions:

1. How unique is the lack of balance in the modern church? Is this a timeless problem? Does it have historical parallels? Or are we living in times the likes of which we have never seen before?

2. How does your sense of the balance of grace and truth in your own faith life compare with that of the world at large? How much are you part of the problem?

3. Why will fixing such problems automatically lead to a more aggressive church? What is it about grace and truth that is anathema to always playing defense in a rogue culture?

4. What is the difference between "freedom" and "license"? Is "freedom" ironically one of the least understood concepts of American Christians?

5. Are you afraid of taking a stand because you'll be exposed of past or ongoing sin, or do you think a willingness to boldly serve the cause of Christ just might be what you need to move you beyond your sin struggles? In other words, why do you think we don't struggle with temptation as much when we're actively serving Christ as we do when we're actively serving ourselves?

Chapter 7

THERE'S NO GOING BACK

It's time to address the elephant in the room.

I've already cowritten a definitive book on the controversy surrounding COVID-19 and the tyranny it inspired called *Faucian Bargain: The Most Powerful and Dangerous Bureaucrat in American History.* While there's no need to rehash that previous work, we cannot ignore it if we're going to successfully impact our culture. That's because COVID-19 is a line of demarcation in America. There was the country and the rules of culture war engagement pre-COVID, and now there's the country and the rules of culture war engagement post-COVID.

There is no going back, either. We're playing for even bigger stakes now. Stakes I want to lay out for you in detail. Here are thirty-two things you need to know about the times in which we live and are called to confront (sorry there's so many, but I hope they're worth your time):

One: COVID has changed the world and the culture war, and we—specifically those of us fighting to conserve America's Judeo-Christian heritage—must change our tactical perspective accordingly. The rules of engagement have changed, and we must respond in kind.

Two: There is this mantra, and maybe it would be more precise to call it a desperate hope, that what happened with COVID is an outlier—such as the tyrannical lockdowns, dishonest data, unprecedented abuses of power, shutting down churches, and so on. This sentiment is often followed by an expressed desire to return to the state of the culture war before COVID. Unfortunately, we never will. While it may be unprecedented, it will not be an outlier. COVID is the omen, pardon the movie pun.

Three: We have shown the Spirit of the Age too much weakness. We have shown it, via COVID, what we never really had with any other culture war issue before this. That if they force us all to personally experience (meaning in our homes and absolutely everywhere we go) the consequences of a contrived crisis (that is really just the Spirit of the Age's quest for power and control), we will dutifully comply.

Four: We all read to our children what will happen if you give a mouse a cookie, so guess what happens when you give the Spirit of the Age this level of instant subservience? It will not be satiated with just this singular infusion of unconditional obedience via COVID. Oh no. It will demand more and more on every front.

Five: Which is why the COVID playbook will be run back on everything moving forward. Insufficient wokeness will be a public health crisis. Guns will be a public health crisis. Your religion, if it refuses to preach the Rainbow Jihad and bow to the Spirit of the Age, will be a public health crisis. We have shown that if they utter these magic words—*public health crisis*—we will assume the position for the Spirit of the Age on demand. After all, you wouldn't want to be one of them there science deniers, would you? You wouldn't want to kill fill-in-whatever-victim-agitprop is being used at this moment, would you? Would you? You wouldn't want to be one of *those* people.

Six: Everything will be made personal to you now. Everything. There will be no more abstract debates or out clauses like "I don't approve that in my life, but who am I to tell someone else how to live?" Nope. Those days are gone forever. You will fully participate in what the Spirit of the Age commands, or you will be condemned and shunned as a bigot with absolutely no in-between.

Seven: You will not be permitted to go anywhere or watch or do anything without being confronted with some demand or request or lecture from the Spirit of the Age that is personal to you. Just as it has marshaled all its combined forces in Washington, DC, Silicon Valley, Hollywood, and Wall Street with COVID, such will be the playbook for all its contrived crises going forward.

Eight: The previous rules of engagement, therefore, which permitted space for people of differing views to still mutually enjoy Americana, are now erased because we showed which rules we would follow unconditionally. And a growing idolatry among our countrymen demands these rules be followed all the more, even as the evidence shows these rules don't work. You would think the more and more data that shows masks don't work and lockdowns don't work would actually humble people to say it was merely the best we could think of at the time. That they're sorry and can't risk any more collateral damage. We've lost cancer screenings, we are sitting on a mental health apocalyptic cliff, and so on and so forth. But there's no humility at all. No self-awareness at all. Just the opposite.

It seems the more the evidence shows these things don't work, the more you are demanded to comply with them.

Nine: The Spirit of the Age has given rise to Karenstan. Being a busybody used to be annoying; now it's virtuous. It's also rather divisive, because all these hall monitors pit us against each other instead of against the Spirit of the Age.

Ten: The Spirit of the Age is a jealous god, and it will not share its glory with another. All of us will choose this day whom we will serve. All will gaze upon the Spirit of the Age and marvel at it, or you will be condemned to second-class citizenry or worse. Take the vaccine passport, bigot.

Eleven: Every culture in all of human history has either worshipped the true Creator of the cosmos or idols. The more our culture rejects its Creator, the more it turns to idolatry, and Spirit of the Age idolatry always turns a culture against itself as various sectarian tribalistic idolatries debate and divide over whose idol is more worthy of being idolized and worshipped.

Twelve: The Spirit of the Age wins either way in this scenario, because unlike our Creator it doesn't unconditionally love us. No, it unconditionally hates us. It shows us fake displays of affection to draw us in by playing to our darkest fears and desires, but once we succumb to its temptations the anti-human, anti-liberty and anti-progress agenda comes forth. That, my friends, is happening right now. Human monkey embryos, anyone? Yeah, that's actually a thing.[6]

Thirteen: The Spirit of the Age claims to offer freedom, but it is peddling bondage instead. Which is proven by the fact you are not free to follow your own

---

6   Nidhi Subbaraman, "First Monkey-Human Embryos Reignite Debate Over Hybrid Animals," *Nature*, April 15, 2021, https://www.nature.com/articles/d41586-021-01001-2.

conscience once the Spirit of the Age has control. There is no freedom of dissent. There is only compliance or the consequences for not giving it.

Fourteen: Folks, the days ahead will create a unique coalition of people opposed to this. At the time this book was being written, I could've given several of atheist Bill Maher's end-of-show rants with very minimal variation beyond taking out the F-bombs. People who were previously opposed to each other, because they thought they had irreconcilable views of what words like "freedom" and "liberty" meant and how far their limits should be pushed, will be realigning as it becomes more obvious the Spirit of the Age plans to ban those ideals altogether.

Fifteen: This new political reality will require activists in our time to be more nimble than our predecessors. Look, we have a two-party system for the most part, whether or not we like it (which I don't, but there's little I can do about it). And yes, I know sometimes it feels as if we don't even really have a second party, let alone the desire for a third one. Nevertheless, as long as that structure remains in place we are going to have to utilize it to some degree to implement our viewpoints as policy. That's just the system we have.

However, unlike previous generations we cannot solely rely upon it. We simply don't even have the numbers within the Republican Party to fully defend our way of life even when Republicans are in power.

Thankfully, though, there are people (including non-white believers) who agree with us on singular issues of fundamental importance yet for various reasons would never cross the partisan picket line to vote Republican to activate with us on them. But if they were given a dedicated opportunity to stand with us beyond the partisan paradigm, they would. This is how we used to pass marriage amendments to state constitutions in blue states like even (gasp!) California. For example, back in 2008 when the state's voters supported a referendum to uphold marriage as one man and one woman, 50 percent of whites voted for it, but 57 percent of non-whites did so.[7]

That's right, defending marriage in California was more popular with non-whites than whites! The same election day that proposition received 53 percent of the vote overall, GOP presidential nominee John McCain only got 37 percent of the state's votes. Marriage, bolstered as a singular issue by non-whites, outperformed the Republican presidential nominee by a whopping 16 points in the bluest of blue states.

The Spirit of the Age knows this, which is why it had to take the marriage issue away from voters and instead hand it to unelected judges. The Spirit of the Age knew that was the only way it was going to be able to nationalize and formalize the final destruction of the American nuclear family. It feared the voters uniting across partisan political lines and in support of first things, so it cleared a path to just bypass the voters altogether. Let's make it fear us along those lines again. Except this time, let's also include reigning in the unbridled power of our black-robed tyrants as part of that unification agenda.

This is the way—strategic discernment. We use the system, instead of continually letting it use us. When we have issues that have a better chance of achieving success by navigating the traditional two-party structure, then do so. And when we're in states and municipalities that permit us to bypass that divisive process and make our

---

7   "Just the Facts: Proposition 8," Public Policy Institute of California, December 2008, https://www.ppic.org/content/pubs/jtf/JTF_Prop8JTF.pdf.

case directly to voters who otherwise wouldn't join with us but agree with us on such points, take full advantage of that, too. Stop putting all our eggs in the GOP basket, especially because it has plenty of holes.

It's a lot easier to convince a majority of people to oppose their kids being taught that men can have a period in a government school if that's the singular issue on the table. Why not invest at least as much energy in that as we do getting a bunch of Republicans who really hate us elected, simply because they're not called Democrats?

What is more important for our children? Putting a few more useless Republicans in the majority to help them pass another tax cut for globalist corporations who fund drag queen story time hour, or taking over the board that oversees the public library to get rid of that filth altogether?

Just as Paul said to the Jew that he was a Jew and to the Greek that he was a Greek to be all things to all people in order to save some of them, we must be partisan when we need to be partisan and be unifying around shared principles when we need to be unifying in order to save as much of our way of life as we can.

When left-wing feminist Naomi Wolf openly supported my efforts to overturn COVID fascism and expose the real data associated with the virus out of a shared desire to get our freedoms back, I joined with her with enthusiasm. Of course, I didn't change my position on any other issue where we disagreed, of which they are numerous and they are vital. But as the Bible says, "Don't muzzle the ox while it's treading its grain." Her support helped the two of us achieve a mutual objective, and I didn't have to compromise anything Christ compels me to stand for in order to obtain it, so why would I ever turn it down? Not to mention the fact it was courageous of her to defy many of her traditional allies in order to stand with the likes of me, so it wouldn't have been very Christ-like of me to shun her for demonstrating such bravery.

We need to not just take yes for an answer, but open up individual opportunities for unbelievers/skeptics like Wolf as well as non-white believers who would never join the GOP to give us yes for an answer, when our mutual interests align.

Maybe I'm missing something, but it's not like we've got so much influence in the culture right now that we can afford to put our overflow supporters on layaway. We're not in a position to look any gift horses in the mouth. We need all the help we can get. Furthermore, what better evangelism opportunity could you ask for than when unbelievers come to us because they preemptively agree with us on something Christ says is important? If that's not a good and natural starting point for that conversation, I don't know what is.

Currently, we're much better at being partisan hacks than we are at achieving our agenda, and the results speak for themselves. Except in very few places, unfortunately, not much really changes regardless of how many Republicans we help get elected. That has to change, or nothing else will.

If we have referendums or local elections that allow us to do so, why should we continually beat our heads against the wall convincing softheaded, gutless, and treacherous Republicans to help us fight the culture war, when there are non-white brethren who would enlist in the fight on several of those breakout issues with us via such a process? If they reject partisanship, offer them this partnership. And it's the perfect antidote to the racialist agenda, critical racist theory, and so forth currently tearing our culture apart at the seams.

Sixteen: The days ahead are no longer about Right versus Left as we have previously known them. Or even nationalism versus globalism as it is described in some circles today. For example, the same Prime Minister Boris Johnson in the United Kingdom who aligned with nationalistic fervor via Brexit was among the worst COVID tyrants in public office in the free world. Where is his nationalism now? Well, authoritarianism became nationalistic, that's where. You give up your way of life because you are a proud Briton, full stop. Because you are a distinguished Englishman is why you bow the knee now to the Spirit of the Age.

Seventeen: The political battle of our era is really now liberty versus tyranny, period. Were we created to be free on any level or not? That. Is. It. That's the whole enchilada. Liberals like Maher disagree with us about the extent of liberty, but they at least agree it must exist. The Spirit of the Age plans to cancel it.

Eighteen: As Christians we understand where true freedom ultimately comes from because it is our sinful state that causes us to impose tyranny on others. That without new life in Christ, we can't help but fall into some state of tyranny as a culture or become some form of bully or despot or villain as individuals.

Nineteen: However, we are becoming aligned now with those who don't fully understand or accept that yet. Perhaps one day they will. I urge you, do not drive them away from the coming coalition. That doesn't mean we deny the Word of God, but it does mean we focus on how best to model it.

Twenty: The reason God uses troubled and problematic people is because, wait for it, *there are only troubled and problematic people.* There is no other kind. All have sinned and fallen short of the glory of God. All of us are long sheep and have gone astray. We are all troubled and problematic. Those willing to join with us for this fight, despite our past and present disagreements, are in my view practicing courage and empathy. We should return it by loving our neighbor as ourselves.

Twenty-one: We once thought as they do now, that we could do things like life, truth, and justice on our own. Again, don't muzzle the ox while it's treading its grain. Don't refuse to take "yes" for an answer. This is a time for critical thinkers of all persuasions to assemble and oppose Thanos snapping away Western civilization, because we are all one snap away from that now.

Twenty-two: Furthermore, COVID has unfortunately shown that plenty of so-called red state public officials can get just as drunk on the tyranny, and you are even seeing some so-called conservatives and libertarians disgustingly proclaim they are fine with the tyranny provided it comes from corporate America instead of the state.

Twenty-three: The truth is, neither side of our long-simmering political debate and culture war can claim the high ground any longer when it comes to the evils of authoritarianism. The oligarchy of cultural elites transcends our past partisan fault lines. We are going to have to oppose big business (traditionally favored by Republicans) just as much as we typically do big government (traditionally favored by Democrats), and vice versa.

Twenty-four: Therefore, it is time to unite critical thinkers from the left, who have a natural distrust of big business, with critical thinkers on the right, who harbor a natural distrust of big government. For the elites are in unity now. They are unified in their shared desire to rule us. Critical thinkers must now be unified in our shared conviction to defy them.

Twenty-five: For believers, as important as it is to forge this new coalition, it is not, and never will be, more important than the Gospel—for nothing ever is. When the moment comes and the time arrives to share the reasons for the hope that we have with our new unbelieving allies and friends, do so with the same courage and empathy that they showed by aligning with us. Seize the moment.

Twenty-six: Be a blessing to this coming coalition, not a hinderance. At the same time, we ultimately represent the Gospel. But does not the Gospel show us there can be unity in our diversity? If any tribe in any nation can confess Jesus is Lord, they can also defend their God-given rights such as life, liberty, and the pursuit of happiness.

Twenty-seven: What better evangelistic platform could we ask for than to bless and coalesce with those who willingly align with God's people to defend the liberty given by the God they either currently reject or don't yet know?

Twenty-eight: However, at the same time we never bury our light under a blanket. We always make it plainly known why we are uniquely in this fight, and what our motivations are for testifying about where true liberty ultimately comes from: "Now the Lord is that Spirit, and where the Spirit of the Lord is, there is liberty."

Twenty-nine: Because in the end, even if this coalition is successful, its success will be limited for now to holding back the Visigoths from coming over the wall. Ultimately, the end game is always the same: revival or bust.

Thirty: Without another Great Awakening that originally gave birth to American freedom and liberty, American freedom and liberty will be lost to history.

Thirty-one: John 3:17 is how we end every show. It says, "God did not send His Son into the world to condemn the world, but so that through Him the world may be saved." This is our time to show the life that is the light of men. We are not ashamed of what we believe, nor are we ashamed of those who do not yet share all our beliefs, but join with us in opposing the evil of Spirit of the Age tyranny.

Thirty-two: Collectively, the men of this era have a long way to go, believer and unbeliever alike. Too often during Covidstan I saw an individual woman or a few mama bears at a school board meeting doing the bulk of the resisting.

Where were all the men?

And no, I'm not talking about the ones trying to bully a homeschool mom about not wearing a useless Chinese face diaper at the drugstore. That's a mere male, or a boy who can shave. I'm talking about the real men, where were they? Where were they even before COVID? You can tell a lot about a culture by the state of its men, and that's a pretty sad state of affairs in early twenty-first-century America.

The number of single women well into their thirties who have emailed me in the past couple of years, desperately yearning for a real man to marry but unable to find one, is heartbreaking. No other generation of American men, especially Christian men, would've tolerated the level of tyranny COVID fascism attempted to impose—let alone willfully and without fuss submitted to it indefinitely. This is a time for men who have read Nehemiah and are prepared to treat modern-day Sanballats accordingly, but too often we're stuck with skinny-jean-wearing, nicer-than-God types.

It was the resolve of Christian men that forged and maintained this nation. Men willing to stand up to tyrants, whether dressed in red coats or swastikas. This nation will dissolve unless this generation of men recovers at least some of that resolve. Try being at least as excited about restoring the Constitution as you are the return of the *NCAA Football* video game. And hey, I love that game, too. But it is just a game. What's threatening your families, or the wife and child you should've had by now, is definitely more than a game. It's as real as real life gets. Try stepping into manhood. You never know—you might actually like it.

Men, we were created to lead. We were created to protect and defend. We were created to serve. And if we were created to do those things, that means our Creator gave us the capability to do those things. Become the hero you were born to be.

Group Discussion Questions:

1. Do you agree that there is no going back to a pre-COVID world? That "getting back to normal" isn't possible or even desirable in some respects? Why or why not?

2. What is the most important thing COVID taught you about the state of the American church and the faith of your fellow Christians both locally and nationally?

3. Have you been personally attacked yet in the name of the Spirit of the Age? If so, how did you respond? If not, why do you think that is? Smart? Lucky? Or perhaps has your witness against lies, propaganda, and blasphemy not been strong enough?

4. Who have you gained the most respect for in cultural and political circles in recent years? Who have you lost the most respect for? Are the reasons related to each other? Why or why not?

5. What is the most important Gospel testimony you think you have to offer to someone who may be open to hearing it for the very first time?

Chapter 8
WITHOUT A VISION THE PEOPLE PERISH

The culture needs THE CHURCH to cast a vision that captures its imagination while competing for its hearts and minds. But does THE CHURCH in contemporary America have such a vision? Without such a vision the American people are perishing as we speak.

Many people—believers and unbelievers alike—don't know what THE CHURCH is and what it does, beyond telling people about Jesus and Heaven and Hell. Unbelievers are unsure that it has the answers they're looking for. Believers read stories from Scripture or church history about how THE CHURCH has changed the world in the past, but they're not sure how to do that today.

What they're both looking for is hope, and THE CHURCH is the only institution that can truly offer hope to this fallen world. Our ultimate hope, of course, is found in Jesus Christ, fully human and yet fully divine. What we're missing, however, is a unified prophetic voice to proclaim who He is and what THE CHURCH that He built is here for and to offer the world.

What the world needs to see from us is transparent transformation. Something that shows them what God has done in our lives, but at the same time makes that change accessible to them as well, just as they are.

Let me tell you a brief a story to illustrate my point.

There once was a master potter who came upon a broken pot of clay that was shattered into several pieces. To most potters it was beyond repair, but this potter was an expert. He could put anything back together again. Slowly but surely he molded the pieces of clay into one, cohesive piece of pottery. It wasn't easy. The work was painstaking. Often the clay didn't want to conform to his will, but the master potter kept at it. Finally he finished with his work, except there was still one problem. Even though the pot was whole again, you couldn't help but notice all the cracks that remained from when it was originally shattered. No matter how much the master potter skillfully molded it, he couldn't get all the cracks out of the clay.

Then one day he had an idea. He needed something to distract outsiders from all the cracks when they looked at the piece of pottery in his display window. So the master potter lit a candle and placed it inside the pot.

Then something amazing happened. As people walked by his shop, they were drawn to this pot with cracks in the clay. Because now, beaming through all the cracks was the refracted light from the candle. The light was so brilliant that it overshadowed the cracks. In fact, the cracks weren't apparent anymore at all, just the light.

Now when people looked at the pot they didn't see cracks, only light. It was that light that drew the people in. What people thought about a broken pot of clay had changed after the inside of the pot changed. It was the change on the inside that attracted people to what was on the outside.

So must it also be with THE CHURCH.

Changed churches change hearts. Changed hearts change people. Changed people change institutions. Changed institutions change communities. Changed communities change the culture.

What prompts that change? What inspires it? Where does it come from? The answer, I believe, is the transforming power of the Word of God. With one prophetic voice THE CHURCH can be that change agent in our nation again by casting a bold and Biblical vision.

Might I suggest one?

Perhaps the bold and Biblical vision THE CHURCH is looking for that will reach this lost generation is found in the sixty-first chapter of the writings of the prophet Isaiah.

It is a vision so powerful that Christ Himself quoted it during His first recorded public ministry appearance in the Book of Luke. It's a vision so inspiring that when John the Baptist's disciples came to him looking for hope while their mentor was awaiting martyrdom in prison, Christ paraphrased it again. Anything Christ says twice has got to be good. This definitely is:

> *The spirit of the Sovereign LORD is upon me, because the LORD has anointed me to preach the good news to the poor. He has sent me to bind up the brokenhearted, to proclaim freedom for the captives, and release from darkness for the prisoners, to proclaim the year of the LORD's favor.*

Within those fifty-three words lies the message that this fallen world is literally dying to hear. Those fifty-three words could provide THE CHURCH with the vision and prophetic voice it lacks in the culture today. Those fifty-three words tell the world exactly who we are and what we do, because when Christ finished reading those words He then looked at all the people in the synagogue and boldly proclaimed, "Today, this is fulfilled among you."

Why was it fulfilled among them? Because Christ was there and that prophecy was about Him. Everywhere Christ went in His earthly ministry those fifty-three words happened.

God in His sovereignty sent Christ to seek and save that which is lost in the power of the Holy Spirit. Christ was anointed to preach the Gospel, or good news, to the poor both materially and in spirit. The material poor would hear Christ speak of charity and demonstrate God's provision, while the poor in spirit would hear Christ say, "I have come so that you may have life, and life abundantly."

He didn't just mourn and weep with those who were brokenhearted; He restored them, sometimes by even raising the dead. Those who were held captive to old ways and old behaviors were reborn and set free from both. Those imprisoned by darkness were released through the light of truth. He proclaimed to the world the time of the Lord's favor, because the Kingdom of God was finally at hand after centuries of waiting for the Messiah's arrival. And when Christ returns to this earth we will finally see the greatest of the Lord's favor of all time.

There's a word that describes what happens to people whose broken hearts have been mended, whose people have been released from captivity and freed from oppression, and who have heard the good news and will never be the same—in Jesus's name. That word is transformed.

We have got to get back to what we do best, and THE CHURCH is at its best when it's about transformation—

of the soul, of the heart, of families, of communities, and of culture. When the Puritans left Holland to travel to England and set sail for the New World, the Dutch government was so upset about losing its best citizens it actually offered them incentives to stay. That's how much those faithful folks had transformed their communities, even though when they first arrived they were legally prohibited from proselytizing the locals. How many of our communities would do the same thing if they found out our churches wanted to relocate to another area?

The Bible's ultimate message is about not just redemption but also transformation. God doesn't just stop at saving us from our sins. He takes it to the next level by replacing our hearts of stone with a heart of flesh. Old things have passed away, and behold all things are made new.

Christ didn't just come to die. He also came to *rise*. And it is the risen Christ who is now ascendant, the ruler of God's creation, and the name by which one day every knee will bow and every tongue will confess that He alone is Lord of all. All power under heaven and earth has been granted to Him, and not even the gates of Hell will prevail against His church.

Shouldn't that give us confidence to fulfill His great commission of discipling the nations? Shouldn't that inspire us to embark upon a mission of transformation? Those fifty-three words of Isaiah 61 symbolize the very definition of Christ's transforming ministry, and I believe they could for ours today as well. I believe those fifty-three words represent the unifying, prophetic voice THE CHURCH is looking for today. Everywhere Christ went those fifty-three words happened. So if we are in Him and He is in us, isn't it safe to say that everywhere THE CHURCH goes those fifty-three words should be happening as well?

When people want to know who is Jesus and what He stands for, point them toward those fifty-three words. When people want to know what THE CHURCH is and what it does, point them toward those fifty-three words. Pastors, when those sitting in the cheap seats need to be reminded why Jesus saved us beyond a need for eternal fire insurance, point us toward those fifty-three words. People, when our pastors get discouraged or need encouragement, point them toward those fifty-three words.

Without a vision the people perish. I believe those fifty-three words cast a vision that could save this nation from perishing.

Group Discussion Questions:

1. How do the reasons people go to church impact the ways the church goes to the world?

2. Are you too ashamed of your brokenness to allow a chance for the light to shine through? Does your testimony even include the depths of your sin?

3. How do twenty-first-century trends and obsessions interfere with and impact the process of individual and cultural transformation?

4. How would your local community react if your church closed tomorrow? If all the churches closed tomorrow?

5. Describe the most beautiful broken pot you've ever met.

Chapter 9
THE SALT AND LIGHT SOLUTION

Now that we've cast a vision, we need an agenda. One that clearly details both our principles and our priorities.

Let's start with laying out some nonnegotiable principles:

Principle #1: There is such a thing as absolute truth.

We are unashamed in publicly proclaiming what the source of our salvation, direction, compassion, character, and integrity is. That source is our personal relationship with Jesus Christ, the Son of the one, true God. So that we may know Him and His ways, God has given us His Word, which is the Bible.

Principle #2: We seek to conform our laws and customs to the "laws of Nature and Nature's God" referenced in our Declaration of Independence—the mission statement of America.

Every culture needs a foundation to start from, and a plumb line to keep it centered. We believe, just as the Founding Fathers did, that both of these are contained within the "laws of Nature and Nature's God." One of the basic revelations of this natural law is found in the Ten Commandments, as just one (but primary) example.

Principle #3: We were created by God to fulfill a specific purpose.

Since God created us, we believe the purpose of life is not merely the pursuit of our own interests. God desires us to live life abundantly, but with His purposes in mind. Now that we have freely received His grace, that purpose is to carry that message of hope to others and our community in both word and deed.

Principle #4: Our adversary is the Spirit of the Age.

We are not contending against flesh and blood, but rather against the principalities, powers, and wicked rulers of this present darkness, as well as spiritual hosts of wickedness in the heavenly places. Or, to put a more contemporary spin on it, the Spirit of the Age—which is the sociopolitical manifestation of the demonic influences wreaking havoc upon our culture. This Spirit of the Age has imprisoned many of our countrymen in its grip, and we seek to free them from it first and foremost.

Principle #5: The God of the Bible is for us, not against us.

God does not place restrictions upon human behavior to be punitive, but instead He does so out of love because He does not want His children hurt and damaged by the impact of sin. And yet when we do turn away, He still welcomes us back unconditionally if we earnestly repent and ask for forgiveness.

Principle #6: Evil is a viable force in the world that must be confronted.

We do not believe that people are essentially good and that our flaws, transgressions, crimes, and unethical behavior can simply be changed for the better by enhancing our environment, improving our financial status, or furthering our education. By themselves, human-created institutions are not completely equipped to deal with what ultimately ails our families, communities, and culture.

Principle #7: A refusal to recognize God's sovereignty unhinges a culture.

We assert the following without wavering: not all beliefs are equal, not all morality is equal, not all cultures are equal, truth is not relative, and ethics are not situational. To the contrary, our contemporary culture says truth is personal to the individual and whatever belief system or behavior is desired at the moment is fine—regardless of its destructive impact—provided a consensus of peers validates it as well. That level of self-indulgence cannot profit a self-governing nation because it ultimately undoes any notion of a unified moral code that binds a people together.

Principle #8: The separation of church and state has gone awry.

We affirm the Constitutional restriction of our government endorsing one faith community over another, particularly in our pluralistic culture. However, this concept has unfortunately led to a near eradication of a Biblical worldview from every vestige of the public and civic arena, and we believe that is contrary to what our Founders originally intended—not to mention contrary to having a healthy society.

Principle #9: Christians placed within positions of cultural leadership should be expected to live out their faith as they lead.

We do not do as the Romans when in Rome, but rather lead by Biblical principles when placed in a position of cultural leadership. Our ultimate citizenship is in the Kingdom of God, and God permits us to be in positions of cultural influence for the expressed purpose of pointing people to the Kingdom of God while we're there.

Now that we have our principles, let's list our priorities:

Priority #1: To promote a culture of truth.

Human beings have a natural yearning to know why they're here on Earth and what the purpose and meaning of life is. The Creator, the God of the Bible, purposefully placed that longing in the hearts of each of us so we would actively seek Him for the answers to life's essential questions. However, in an increasingly secularized and relativistic culture, such as ours that promotes truth as personal and not transcendent, that quest can lead to destructive detours. A culture is always better served by recognizing and acknowledging God's sovereignty as opposed to trusting in human wisdom and institutions alone.

Priority #2: To promote a culture of compassion.

Human beings have no greater need than to be loved, and they will go to great lengths to fulfill it. The love every human being is ultimately searching for can be found only in an intimate relationship with the God of the Bible. As believers we are required to spread the Good News of Christ to the lost. The most effective and joyful way of doing that is following His commandment to love our neighbors as ourselves and following His lead in serving others.

Priority #3: To promote a culture of life.

Human beings are much more than evolutionary accidents and cosmic coincidences. They are created in the image and likeness of the God of the Bible, who is the lone source of life, with a specific purpose in mind. It is clearly against God's will for human beings to disregard the sanctity of life, especially by shedding innocent blood, and as a result it has a debilitating moral impact on any culture that does so. A culture is always better served by seeking the sovereign God's definition of life as opposed to one it manufactures on its own.

Priority #4: To promote a culture of integrity.

Human beings were created by the God of the Bible to be free, but not with the intent of indulging their sinful natures. God does not seek limits on human behavior to be punitive, but instead so that His children can avoid the harmful results of sin. Sin separates us from God and His plan for mankind, and thus has drastic and destructive consequences. All human beings are born into sin and are only freed from that bondage through a relationship with the risen Christ. A culture is always better served by recognizing why God seeks to keep His children away from potentially harmful behaviors, as opposed to simply enabling or incentivizing the behavioral appetites of the people at the time.

Priority #5: To promote a culture of justice.

Human beings, created in the image and likeness of the God of the Bible, long to see good rewarded and evil punished. Despite our ingrained sin and the shifting sands of contemporary culture, we still readily identify right from wrong. This is a characteristic emblematic of our Creator, who alone is the perfect balance between grace and truth and mercy and judgment. A culture is always better served by following God's examples of restitution, accountability, and restoration as a means of keeping the peace, as opposed to subjecting itself to vengeance, relativism, and leniency. The rights of victims come first, and they must be made whole and restored before restoration is granted to the perpetrator. And some crimes can be so heinous that restoration in this life just isn't possible.

If there's a central premise to both these priorities and purposes, it can be found in these words from President Abraham Lincoln during the Civil War:

> *My concern is not whether God is on our side, my greatest concern is to be on God's side for God is always right.*[8]

---

8   Joe Carter, "Being on God's Side: An Open Letter to the Religious Right," *First Things*, December 22, 2010, https://www.firstthings.com/web-exclusives/2010/12/being-on-gods-side-an-open-letter-to-the-religious-right.

Group Discussion Questions:

1. *Que est veritas* (what is truth)? Do people make you feel ashamed if theirs is different from yours? Is that why we remain silent?

2. If the Founders were obviously talking about the primacy of both reason and revelation when they penned "the laws of Nature and Nature's God," why have emotional virtue signaling, victimology, and the separation of church and state been such seductive usurpers of the American plumb line?

3. How often during a typical day do you contemplate the work of either God or the devil in your life? Is your prayer life offensive or defensive in nature?

4. How are compassion and tolerance different? Which do/should Christians tend to practice more?

5. How are justice and utopia different? Which do/should Christians tend to aspire to more?

Chapter 10
RULES FOR DEFIANCE

It is now time to talk about how to go back on offense. It is time now for some Rules for Defiance, because make no mistake—all of us are going to have to defy the Spirit of the Age.

Rule #1: Assume you are being lied to.

Assume that the system you're up against is lying to you about everything. Absolutely. Everything. Truth is chloroformed in real time in our culture, so practice discernment and assume every narrative you are fed—no matter from which direction—is a lie. Of course, they're really not all lies, mind you. But just to be on the safe side, start there to prevent getting duped. Like in Little League, when you're taught to step back on any fly ball to the outfield before charging in, because it's easier to run forward than recover backwards.

Rule #2: Take being informed more seriously than ever before, because it's harder than ever before.

Fill the vacuum left by rejecting fake news narratives with the best information you can find. Remember, there is wisdom (a bestselling book once said) in a multitude of council. Rely on as many sources as you can. That's what I do. If you look at my Twitter feed, it's a hodge-podge and motley crew of news sources from various political perspectives. I pit them against each other every day as I begin formulating where I get my own information to do my show. I recommend you do the same. Play them off one another. See if there is verifiable information you can rely on within more than one source. And don't just fall for outlandish clickbait that suits your narrative, either. Trust me, there're plenty of grifters on "our side" who want to take advantage of you, too. Don't fall for it.

Rule #3: Maintain meekness, or power under control.

Before we take back our power as a people we need to remember how to wield it. We don't throw tantrums. In our anger we do not sin. Instead, we let our anger motivate us to righteous action. We don't seek vengeance. We do not hate. That does not mean we aren't aggressive or nonconfrontational. If you listen to my show for ten minutes you will accuse me of many things, but nonconfrontational will not be one of them.

It does not mean we are unwilling to boldly and unapologetically stand for what we believe, but remember that we are to be the antidote to the poison rotting our culture. Not simply a different poison. Poison times poison is just more poison. Zero times zero is just more zero. We aren't the Bolsheviks versus the Mensheviks or vice versa. There's no winner in that fight. Everyone's a loser. Nor can we be the mob storming the Bastille to unleash a Reign of Terror later on. Maintain control of our frustration and our anger. Trust that we will be empowered to do bold deeds when we are under control.

Rule #4: Never abandon your motivations.

The Lord chastens those whom He loves. We discipline our children because we love them. In both cases, the motivation for correction—even when it is stern—is to bring people to repentance or redemption or restoration, whichever terminology you prefer. I kind of like all those words. We don't want to annihilate our neighbors. We want to win them. Therefore, our tactics need to never undermine our motivations.

Rule #5: Know thy enemy (and hint...it's probably not your neighbor—even that really annoying one.)

The real enemy here is the Spirit of the Age. A demonic manifestation of forces seeking to end Western civilization as it has been known for centuries. American Exceptionalism is just the latest variant, if you will, of Western civilization. Many of those who are plugged into the Matrix and annoying the heck out of us right now don't know that they are actually being victimized. I got a great note once from a gentleman who gave our book *Faucian Bargain* to a liberal neighbor of his whom he liked. He was sad to see him afraid of his own shadow as he double- and triple-masked his life away.

So one day he said, "Brother, just do me a favor. You read this, give me one of your crazy books, and I'll read it if you want. I'll trade you. Just read this, and if you find something you think is factually inaccurate, bring it to my attention, but other than that I hope it helps you."

His neighbor read it, and little by little his neighbor is outdoors without a mask and hanging out doing stuff with his kids again. See, the Son of Man came to seek and save that which is lost. Thus, that's also what we are trying to do here. A good disciple seeks to emulate his Master. We want to free people from the Spirit of the Age and encourage them to be free as they were created to be.

Rule #6: Feed the sheep and confront the wolves.

Mercy triumphs over judgment for the sheep. However, we give no quarter to the wolves. How do you know the difference between the two?

Sheep just don't know any better; they are ignorant/innocent creatures in need of a shepherd. But wolves don't want to know any better. They know what they are doing. They know who they are. Sheep are deceived, but wolves are willful deceivers. Confronting wolves is how we set the captives free, and the wolves will devour the sheep if we don't. Remember Augustine's charge—there are many sheep without but many wolves within.

Rule #7: Civil disobedience is required by us now to hopefully avoid civil war for our children later.

Our culture is headed down a road to nowhere, which is exactly what the Spirit of the Age that loathes us wants. It doesn't care if it is globalism, progressivism, patriotism, nationalism, or any other "ism"; as long as it drags us down into the pit, the Spirit of the Age is gleeful.

If we don't peaceably but aggressively act on what we believe now, history teaches we may be forced to act on it in ways that inflict much more collateral damage later. I would like to avoid that. I think many of you would like that, too. So we defy now to avoid division later.

Civil disobedience to tyrants is obedience to God.

Government does not own our breath, so burn that useless Chinese face diaper and never again grant government permission to impose a hijab. Government is not owed our unconditional allegiance. We only render unto Caesar that which is Caesar's. When the state asks something of us that only belongs to God, we have a simple answer—no.

If we are not prepared to tell the state that single word now, and face the consequences for doing so head-on as we stand in the gap for what's left of our way of life, then our children and grandchildren will face much worse later.

Rule #8: We need to come together.

A triple-braided cord is tougher to break. We are better together. We were meant to be together. Therefore, we should push back together. Class-action lawsuits. Not one church or one parent by themselves. Acts of mass defiance to both big government and big business, whichever seeks to impose the coercive will of the Spirit of the Age. Not just singular free agents that can be scared off or carried off. Work together. Coordinate together. Serve together. Show the Spirit of the Age there are more of us than it thought. One teacher who refuses to teach anymore pagan indoctrination mythology or critical racist theory in his class can be fired, but what if fifty or a hundred of you in just a single state refused to do so? Would they dare fire you all considering all the blowback that could result? Let's find out, because that's how we create change. Change doesn't happen by just being comfortable, but by being comfortable making oppressors uncomfortable. Do this and you might be surprised how many of your friends and family may later want to join the side that is winning, despite being too scared to join now.

Rule #9: Shame the shamers.

Right now the Spirit of the Age gets to act with impunity no matter how ridiculous or despotic it may be. That needs to change. Bullies only stop when they're forced to learn they bleed, too. The bully's perceived power comes from the confidence nobody will confront them.

Take that confidence away. Act on the confidence of your convictions instead. Make the bullies infamous. Take the mask off the Spirit of the Age and show the world what is truly underneath that kilt. Let everyone see beyond the threats and name-calling that there simply is no "there" there. It's all bluster. Sound and fury, signifying nothing.

This will likely require a form of suffering at some point for some of us. We must be willing to pay the price the Spirit of the Age will attempt to inflict upon some of us for daring to defy it.

The story of Telemachus, the monk credited with ending the gladiator games in ancient Rome, is an example of this. He stood up to protest the ghoulishness of the gladiator games and was murdered by the mob for it. However, the savagery of his murder so appalled Rome that it eventually did lead to the end of the gladiator games.

Then there are followers of the civil rights movement of twentieth-century America. They faced lynching, high-pressure water hoses, and incarceration. How about the signers of the Declaration of Independence, who pledged their "lives, fortunes, and sacred honors"? Several of them paid that price to give birth to America.

Finally, the ultimate example is our Lord. He underwent a gruesome torture and execution to defeat the last enemy and fulfill the wrath of the Father. His apostles picked up their Cross and followed Him, too.

The message to us is clear. We will not be able to defeat the Spirit of the Age without a willingness to risk suffering for the cause. We cannot go on offense against the Spirit of the Age without offending it. When tyrants are offended they tend to lash out. But be of good cheer. Our Lord has overcome the world, which is why His name is still celebrated and worshipped by billions two thousand years later, while the remains of centuries of tyrants have been rotting in the ground.

Rule #10: Make red states/communities red again.

Balkanize even further. Unless you are being specifically called into domestic missions, purposefully move to places where fellow believers are concentrated. When you get there, or if you already are there, make that red state/community the absolute reddest it's ever been. To the point you are as red as California is blue, and then make sure to elect local/state officials who will maintain that status.

California didn't care if George W. Bush or Donald Trump was president. It remained firmly ensconced in the Twilight Zone regardless. Likewise, you don't care if Joe Biden or Karl Marx himself lives at the White House because you ain't changing your way of life one bit. You have the numbers, and leverage wins.

But what about evangelizing the lost? Keep in mind, many of the church leaders who will issue that objection entirely out of context also preside over ministries with no real cultural impact whatsoever—as evidenced by the increasing paganization of the culture surrounding them. Furthermore, nowhere in the Scriptures does it say our children and families are to be pawns in a culture war. In fact, it actually urges us to protect the youth from such influences. Cite me the passage where Paul urges believers to expose their children to pagan indoctrination in the hopes they'll be crusading evangelists at age eight. That's what I thought.

There are lots of ways to evangelize without risking our families as collateral damage. Instead of taking mission trips overseas, take one to California or New York. They're essentially foreign countries now. Another way of evangelizing, modeled by the Puritans, was showing the dominant culture a superior way of life. Their countercultural living revitalized Christendom and even galvanized the founding of this country.

I'm not Amish or Mennonite. I happen to like technology and internal combustion engines. I'm not suggesting shutting ourselves off from the outside world whatsoever. For goodness sake, I work in digital broadcasting. Thus, modern technology and reaching a broad and diverse audience is sort of my jam.

I am suggesting no longer allowing the outside world to dictate to us how much of our worldview we can live out. Why did the Pilgrims risk their lives on the *Mayflower*? Because they were out of options to live their beliefs in their native country. We, however, are not out of those options. There are still plenty of places across the country, even plenty of counties within blue states, where we have overwhelming numbers to ensure our liberty.

So use it or lose it.

Rule #11: Take "yes" for an answer.

Accept assistance and support from nontraditional sources and people, including those who have vehemently disagreed with us in the past and may still now on fundamental issues. Accept apologies and reconciliation with those who previously were citizens of Karenstan and want out. Do not muzzle the ox while it is treading its grain (yeah, I said it again). Whoever is for us at this moment isn't against us, and whoever isn't against us at this moment is for us. Take "yes" for an answer. Because our list of allies grows thin, Aragorn.

Speaking of which, all of you reading this right now need to acknowledge that it is time for you to be Aragorn. You have hidden out like a ranger, doing random acts of principled voting or other stealth activisms for far too long. Maybe even putting something on social media or talking to a neighbor now and then.

But you've been on the outskirts of where the fire really rages the hottest. And part of it is because you may be afraid to step into that light. *Do I have what it takes? Can the answer really be me? Can I really be a change agent?* Somebody told me recently a family member told them that one person can't make a difference. They obviously haven't ever read a history book.

I'm your Elrond. I'm handing you the sword of the king you've been unwilling to take ownership of for far too long. You are all called to be Aragorns, the people in a country where the people rule. Take the sword, step into your legacy, and become the American people you were meant and born to be before it's too late.

Group Discussion Questions:

1. How could THE CHURCH be doing more to correct the problem of disinformation and propaganda in our media culture?

2. Have you had any personal success growing closer to/changing the viewpoint of someone you previously thought was impossible to make any kind of connection with? If so, how did you do it?

3. Is it more difficult for you to give mercy to sheep or to give no quarter to wolves? Is allowing one to grow out of proportion with the other a form of personal idolatry?

4. Why does civil disobedience seem to be viewed as a mortal sin for many "Christians," particularly since we begin teaching school children about Martin Luther King Jr. in kindergarten?

4. Making red states red again will require you to get outside of your comfort zone and perhaps even suffer. Are there aspects of your current life defined by a certain "gated community effect" that keep you from going to Nineveh as you should? Are you addicted to comfort more than you would like to admit?

Chapter 11
SHARE YOUR STORY AND LET PEOPLE IN

Recently I was speaking at a national conference in Idaho with believers in attendance from thirty-eight states. During the Q&A portion of the discussion, a young man from Los Angeles got up and asked me for a detailed plan on how to impact his community for the Kingdom. The answer I gave may have surprised him.

I said that after more than a decade in full-time activism, I could happily provide him with a plan. One of my previous books, *Rules for Patriots: How Conservatives Can Win Again*, does just that. However, given the fact our culture is currently crumbling at the molecular level, we need something that's more granular than grandeur.

Therefore, I told him and the audience to start with something very basic. So I began asking questions. Basic questions. Is your church even open? Is your home even open? Do your unbelieving family, friends, and neighbors know that, despite your unwillingness to go along with the Spirit of the Age like many of them are, you are open for business if they're in the market for a new way of life?

Are you a (pardon the expression) safe space if they're in trouble? Are you a port in the storm of life when they feel caught in the undertow? Can they go to you knowing you'll stand in the gap for them? Do you love them because God first loved you?

I once heard the late D. James Kennedy say, "The one thing you'll never find in the Bible is an evangelism plan." Perhaps that's because there is no better plan than loving your neighbor as you love yourself. I think this realization particularly energizes the potential for success among those of us who are faith-based activists as well. It helps us demonstrate we're not here just to impose our political beliefs on others, but we have these political beliefs precisely because we love our neighbor as we love ourselves.

Nothing is more precious in God's sight than people. Theology is vitally important, yes, but Jesus ultimately died for people and not a theology. And we don't want to see people destroyed by straying too far from the laws of Nature and Nature's God. Those laws are there specifically for our protection, similar to how we as loving parents don't let our children play with electrical outlets or in traffic in order to protect them from danger. We don't put those restrictions in place and then punish them for violating them because we don't love our children—*but precisely because we do.*

However, if all we did with our children was hold them accountable to a righteous standard, would that not increase the odds they'd grow to resent that standard and rebel against it later? Holding people, or the culture, to a righteous standard is only part of the equation. Acts of service, or demonstrating our love for others in humble and tender ways, complete the circle. Is God a god of justice or mercy? The answer is yes. Is God a god of retribution or redemption? Again, the answer is yes.

For example, which is a righteous form of pro-life activism? Spending a Saturday outside a child-killing clinic and praying for the women to turn away before it's too late, and/or directly urging them not to go through with it? Or providing adoption services or assistance for unwed mothers so they know the support is there if they turn from the darkness and step into the light? Once more, the answer is yes.

It's not the carrot *or* the stick, it's the carrot *and* the stick.

I saved this part of the discussion for toward the end of this book because what's lacking more than anything in our cultural engagement is courage of conviction. That's why we've spent the preponderance of our time addressing that crisis. But now that we're coming to the close here, let us not become activists for activism's sake. Instead, let us do everything for Christ's sake. If our focus is on doing whatever we're doing for Christ—and that would be the Christ in the Bible, not the one conjured by our vain imaginings or cultural stereotypes—then we shouldn't struggle with whether to be the type of people who turn over money changers or befriend sinners.

We'll be both.

The same Jesus who said on the Cross while being tortured, "Father forgive them for they know not what they do," is the same Christ who will return one day with a sword in His mouth and a robe dipped in blood looking to take names.

Jesus perpetually remains the baby born in the humble manger at Christmastime for much of our culture. He's always cute and cuddly, just looking to love on people right where they're at. And while we are right to reject that false premise, let us also not risk completely disregarding the fact that God incarnate did choose to come to earth that way.

For everything there is a time and a season. There is a time to humbly show people the Kingdom of God, and then there is a time to remind them it is wise to reverentially fear Almighty God, too. It's not about which we should be, but when. Do we feed sheep or confront wolves?

Hopefully by now you guessed it, the answer is yes.

Relationships are key here. While it's become a cliché to say people won't care about what you know until they know how much you care—to the point it's become an excuse to never speak up and confront a wayward culture—that doesn't mean it's not true in its original context. When Nicodemus came to meet with Christ privately, did Jesus reject him as one of the "blind guides" of religious leaders He repeatedly and publicly criticized? No, just the opposite. When Nicodemus made the move to open the door to a relationship, Christ walked through it. At the same time, He didn't suddenly go soft on the Sanhedrin just because one of its esteemed members had reached out to Him, either.

If it sounds like Christlikeness requires a nimbleness that doesn't come naturally to us, well, you're right. That's why we need to be new creations! Some of us are predisposed to love until we're fully taken advantage of and manipulated, and some of us are prone to confront at the first sign of opposition. But those would be *our* natures, and we are called to show this lost world *His* nature.

The same God who made a Heaven also permitted a Hell, and vice versa.

Along those lines, part of letting people in also requires a new level of transparency. First Corinthians is one of Paul's sternest letters. The city of Corinth was especially depraved, even by first-century Greco-Roman lascivious standards. In fact, if you were especially licentious in those days you were known to "Corithianize." Corinth was so brazen, even the carnal Greeks made them a nickname.

It's within this wayward city that Paul planted a church. Not surprisingly, a church planted within a pagan mecca faces some challenges. There's the dude in the front row with his arm around his stepmom, then there're the folks who keep getting in line to get drunk off the communal wine, and then there's all the hefty community baggage brought into the ministry from the members living there. Paul spares no sacred cows in confronting the immorality and false teaching invading the church in Corinth, but in the midst of that old-time religion he also says this:

> *Or do you not know that the unrighteous will not inherit the Kingdom of God? Do not be deceived: neither the sexually immoral, nor idolaters, nor adulterers, nor men who practice homosexuality, nor thieves, nor the greedy, nor drunkards, nor revilers, nor swindlers will inherit the Kingdom of God.* ***And such as once were some of you.*** **[emphasis added]**

That last sentence in bold is key to this conversation. Paul is making it very clear the outside pagan influences are a road to nowhere, but then he reminds the believers in Corinth they were once captives to the exact same darkness. What set them free? Paul reminds them of that, too, next:

But you were washed, you were sanctified, you were justified in the name of the Lord Jesus Christ and by the Spirit of our God.

In other words, the believers in Corinth aren't *better* people than the pagans surrounding them; they're *different* people. And what made them different? Their restored relationship with their Creator through the atonement offered through His son, Jesus Christ, that's what. Take that away, and you are no different than that which you are against. In fact, you're probably not even against these things at all.

This also means all of us have a testimony, a story to tell, about the wretches we once were. **Do not withhold your story.** Now, don't be proud of it per se, but it's okay to brag on your God a bit and be proud of the work He's done to set you free from your sin. That story, your testimony, is what connects you to the people you're trying to impact. We've been where they are. We can relate to what they're struggling with, **for such as once were some of us.**

This is one of the two main reasons I'm so honest about my personal story and ongoing personal struggles on my show and in public. The other is to warn people against making me your new idol to replace the old ones who already let you down, for I'll let you down, too. That's just what idols do. I didn't cease being human. You don't want to know what I'm thinking all the time, trust me. People make for terrible heroes, but regular people made in the image of an Almighty God can do heroic things.

How did a kid born to a fifteen-year-old mom like me get here? I flunked out of college, which is apparently what happens when you don't attend a class for an entire semester but just party and play Super Tecmo Bowl instead. I met my wife in an old AOL dial-up hook-up chatroom. We never intended to get married, let alone stay married and even homeschool our kids. It also hasn't been easy staying married. We're both sinners, and it's hard living with each of us. There were moments we thought this thing was over, some of them recently, but here we are going on twenty-five years.

I'm not always a perfect parent. I love my kids with all I have, and they love me as well; but we don't always agree, and there're times they've seen me behave hypocritically. I have a good relationship with each of them, but I'm not sure all three of them will end up believing the same as the old man. Or at the very least won't have to build their own testimonies on the road to getting there.

I grew up in an abusive home, primarily because of the demons haunting my stepdad from his own dysfunctional upbringing. I currently have no relationship with my biological father, who was also a teenager when I was born, after repeated attempts over the years. My teenage mom, with whom I've always been close, was scared she couldn't raise a child and considered aborting me after *Roe v. Wade*.

I was hardly a virgin on my wedding night. It's hard for me not to notice every woman in yoga pants at the gym to this day. I grew up in America's porn generation and have been exposed to more of it than I care to admit. I want to prey upon my enemies far more than pray for them.

And did I mention I'm a Detroit Lions fan? That's right, baby, just one playoff win since 1958! So clearly self-loathing is another one of my many maladies.

Needless to say, I've got a lot of issues.

And yet, here I am. Frontline culture warrior broadcasting on one of the largest platforms in the country each weekday. Nearly every day somebody sends me a note about how my show has positively impacted their faith or maybe even inspired it. How can this be? It's pretty clear I'm a freaking wreck.

Casting Crowns said it best in one of my favorite contemporary Christian songs:

Not because of who I am, but because of what you've done.
Not because of what I've done, but because of who you are.

See, while I'm no hero, I am someone through whom God in His sovereignty has chosen to do some heroic things. **And such as once are each of you.** Not because of who I am, as if I'm someone special, but because of what He's chosen to do with my life. And not because of what I've done to earn that level of favor, but because of who God is to grant it. This whole thing isn't riding on my character or gifts—it's riding on His.

It's now time for each of you take that ride as well. All you need to do to get started is share your story and let people in.

Group Discussion Questions:

1. When it comes to serving Christ by loving our neighbor as we love ourselves, what preaching do you need to hear more of in church to make that happen? What preaching is getting in the way of that? What ministries do you need more of to make that happen? What ministries are getting in the way of that?

2. What balance/dichotomy was being referred to above with the statement "It's not about which we should be, but when"? Define the terms as clearly as possible so you never forget them. How will you proceed according to those terms in the future?

3. Are you too ashamed to talk about your struggle with sin? Can Christ truly be your light if you are? Are you a Christian because you think you are a better person, or are you a better person because you are a Christian?

4. What would be impossible in your current life without Christ? Do you spend too much time thinking you are Paul the Apostle without ever remembering you were once Saul of Tarsus?

5. What is good? What is true? What is beautiful? Will you fight for it? Will you die for it? Will you love for it?

Conclusion

REVIVAL OR BUST

Let's face it, we've been sold a lot of platitudes packaged as principles, soul-less partisanship sold as political activism, and fake news presented as the news.

The temptation to eject from the public square altogether and erect compounds/monasteries to insulate us from the rampaging Spirit of the Age is one I wrestle with—and I get paid to be in the fight. I can't even imagine what someone like most of you reading this who aren't are thinking at this point in our nation's history. How you don't just shut us all off in frustration, because you just get all wound up and nothing changes, and then go and live your own lives as best you can.

I'm not going to finish this book with more empty rhetoric about how America's best days are still ahead, because I'm not so sure about that. I don't know how anyone who actually believes in what America was originally founded upon could honestly say such a thing. Nor am I going to falsely prophesy about how the upcoming election is "the most important election of our lifetimes." Typically when a politician says this the subliminal meaning is "Dang skippy it's the most important election of our lifetimes—particularly mine. I don't want to have to lose and then get a real job, you know like get an office down the street from the capitol and become a lobbyist."

I have worked full-time in politics either as an organizer, activist, strategist, pundit, or commentator for going on a second decade now. And trust me when I tell you, if you think you're too cynical you're probably not cynical enough.

By this point you're probably thinking, *Golly, Steve, this is trending to be the most downer conclusion ever.* Quite the contrary, though I know at this moment it may not seem like it, my intent is to simply make it among the most honest.

On several occasions in this book I have attempted to inspire and motivate, or motivate and inspire. But now that we've come to the end of the training portion of this exercise and stuff is about to get real, I think we need to close with one last dose of realism before sending you out as sheep among wolves.

Jesus warned His own disciples of the cost they would pay to follow Him, and of course He was right. They were all, but one, martyred and often brutally so. The lone escapee of that fate was still tortured and left to die alone.

The soldiers on all those fleets of boats approaching Normandy that June morning were well aware of the fact that the odds were high either they or the man next to them wasn't going to live to see the next sunrise.

And yet, in each of those cases, that level of commitment changed the world—even if those who achieved it didn't always live to see the fruits of their labors. In a letter sent to his wife, Abigail, late in the Revolutionary War, Founding Father John Adams laid down the gauntlet with these words:

> The science of government it is my duty to study, more than all other sciences; the arts of legislation and administration and negotiation ought to take the place of, indeed exclude, in a manner, all other arts. I must study politics and war, that our sons may have liberty to study mathematics and philosophy.[9]

This is the charge we must take up in our time. It is left to our generation to, as St. Paul put it, "set aside childish things." That doesn't mean we can't still enjoy the benefits of being an American and the blessings that still exist here, which we probably no longer deserve. But we need to reassess our priorities.

The hour is late. The clock is ticking. The window is closing. We need, at the very least, a little less complacency and a little more courage of conviction around here. Otherwise we risk cursing our children and grandchildren with being the terminal generation of not just American Exceptionalism—but Western civilization altogether.

If this book convinced you to come this far, I'm guessing you already know this and you're ready to do something. Run for your local school board, or at least annoy it. Encourage your pastor to be bolder, or become that pastor. Take truth-seeking and critical thinking far more seriously and then unapologetically share that truth with others. And so on and so forth.

---

9   John Adams to Abigail Adams, letter, May 12, 1780, *Adams Family Papers*, Massachusetts Historical Society, https://www.masshist.org/digitaladams/archive/doc?id=L17800512jasecond.

However, I think one more thing needs to be said before we close this book. And I wouldn't be completely honest with you if I didn't say it.

We could do everything right, or even better and beyond what I'm capable of articulating in this book or on my show, and we still might "lose." This culture could still fade to black. This country could still be catapulted upon the ash heap of history.

We could still go bust.

It isn't just that the culture just hasn't heard it or just doesn't know it, nor is it just that we've been largely ineffective in recent history sharing and showing it. Those things are factors in why we're on the brink for sure, and I've spent a good deal of time highlighting them in this book because frankly they're the only things we can control. We can only control if they hear it, if they know it, or if we share it and show it better. We cannot control what the results of doing those things better will be.

We need to acknowledge from the outset here that there's at least a reasonable chance this culture is too far gone to turn back now. That there is no clever or creative way to point this culture to the way, because this culture's answer is already a firm "no way." There's a reasonable chance here that pharaoh has hardened his heart, so to speak.

We don't know that for sure, but I do know this for sure—there is only one way to find out. And that's to go and try to make disciples.

But just know up front not to get discouraged if we still "lose." I heard a powerful message about this early in my faith walk from the late Adrian Rogers. He was telling a story about his first attempt at marching on the gates of hell, and how it left him discouraged when not as many people responded as he had hoped. Rogers talked about how he expressed his dejection to God and then even challenged God by saying he was gonna randomly open his Bible to a page, and if what he saw didn't immediately speak to the discouragement he was feeling, he might hit the eject altogether.

So Rogers did exactly that, randomly opening his Bible and looking down to see if it would speak to his current plight. When he looked down, he saw these words from Ezekiel 33:

> As for you, son of man, your people who talk together about you by the walls and at the doors of the houses, say to one another, each to his brother, "Come, and hear what the word is that comes from the LORD." And they come to you as people come, and they sit before you as my people, and they hear what you say but they will not do it; for with lustful talk in their mouths they act; their heart is set on their gain. And behold, you are to them like one who sings lustful songs with a beautiful voice and plays well on an instrument, for they hear what you say, but they will not do it. When this comes—and come it will!—then they will know that a prophet has been among them.

That will certainly get your attention, won't it? Rogers went on to spend decades in the pulpit, including three terms as president of the Southern Baptist Convention, before his death in 2005. The lesson Rogers learned from this moment is ultimately it is simply his job to deliver the message, but outcomes are up to God. I pray you will internalize that lesson as well before you step out on faith and step into the arena.

Several years ago I was asked to speak to TeenPact, an outstanding organization that helps equip Christian young adults who have expressed an interest for a future in politics. Yet after watching the presentation prior to my speaking slot, I grew concerned these young adults weren't being truly told what it was going to take to impact the political system for Christ. Like when we take Jeremiah 29:11 out of context, when we love God's encouraging word in that singular verse but forget it is surrounded by whole sections of God pronouncing and carrying out judgment against His own people.

So as someone who actually knew several of the state legislators and politicos who had given these young adults the whitewashed/scrubbed presentation, I decided it was time someone shared with them the full measure of what they're up against. So I asked them if they felt they had a real handle on how Iowa's legislature works after spending a day seeing it up close. Of course the group earnestly answered in the affirmative.

"Did they take you up to the fancy steakhouse downtown and let you see the lobbyists buy your legislators steak and martini lunches? Because that's how stuff really gets done around here," I then told them.

The room fell silent, but I noticed the young adults were paying even more attention now. Almost as if they suspected they were being denied some knowledge they needed to know, and now it was upon them.

After I finished my talk I went back to my studio to prepare for my show. That's when I received an irate email from one of the TeenPact organizers, who basically accused me of polluting these young impressionable minds. When I asked him if he could point me to something I said to the group that wasn't true, I received no reply.

Now, keep in mind, these are not children but young adults. Many of them almost finished with high school. All of them granted by their Creator the biological capability to make a baby, so perhaps that at least implies that God no longer considers they need to be babied? I'll even grant the point I can be a tad gruff. I know, you're all very surprised with this disclosure; thus, I admit perhaps someone else could've said what I did better.

But this TeenPact guy didn't want it said at all. In my opinion, that would leave these young adults either woefully unprepared for the task at hand or dangerously naïve to the point of being grist for the Spirit of the Age mill once they arrived on the scene. Chewed up and spit out because they thought they were feeding sheep when they needed to be prepped to confront wolves.

Either way, it means we have failed them. Here, at the end of our time together, I didn't want to fail you. Which is why we all need to understand, despite our best and most noble efforts to save the patient, the Spirit of the Age cancer may have metastasized too much. But at the very least, let us do our best to find out. Because who knows, perhaps a merciful God will see our efforts and grant a culture undeserving of it even more of His bountiful mercy? Maybe a God who specializes in resurrections has another one up His sleeve?

Which brings us to revival.

Minus revival, this thing we call these United States of America is toast, and likely soon. The center cannot hold. A house divided cannot stand. Light and dark cannot mix. Ultimately, I believe the Scriptures and church history teach us revival is exclusively the jurisdiction of God alone. However, I wonder if we could move the heart of God accordingly? Is there a way to demonstrate our sincere desire for it?

I'm not a theologian; I've never been to seminary. I'm not a pastor; I frankly lack the personal holiness and patience necessary for that gig. I didn't even stay at a Holiday Inn Express last night. Nevertheless, since pontification and projection are part of my job, let me close this book by doing some of those here.

I believe it is possible we could convince God of our sincere desire for revival if we do two things—repentance and reformation.

When you really boil it down, all the Christian life is a life of repentance. A recognition of the tremendous toll Christ paid for you to not die the death you should've died, and pay the penalty for your sins you should've paid. That produces a spirit of humility or a recognition that our lives are not our own; we were bought (see that as redeemed) at a high price.

What if we committed ourselves to a life of repentance? Of admitting our mistakes and failures? Of owning up to them—past, present, and future? What if we sought forgiveness for those we've hurt and forgave those who have hurt us? What if we gave one another the benefit of the doubt more often instead of canceling them? What if we killed each other with kindness instead?

What if mercy triumphed over judgment?

That's not to say judgement is now forever absent, because a holy God ultimately demands justice. But what if our default was to love one another out of a recognition that we also have so much to repent for, instead of hiding our struggles while looking to condemn others for theirs? At the very least, then could we say that if judgment still must come, it's because those who refused a life of repentance and the mercy that goes along with it brought it on themselves.

Then there's reformation. Now capital R Reformation was one of the most historically significant events of all time, regardless of which side of the theological divide you currently reside. But in this case I'm talking about small r reformation, which I would define as worshipping God in the manner He commands and deserves. Not the manner we decide. That we give God the same faithful offering Abel did, rather than the shallow or rote or selfish offering his murdering brother Cain did.

For example, what if we didn't consider the church music (which we often refer to as worship) on the basis of what best appeals to the masses but what best glorifies God in this present age?

What if we just opened up the Word of God from the pulpit and let it speak for itself, with pastors who only sought to provide contemporary applications of its timeless truths as opposed to politically correct clarifications?

What if we actually believed the ultimate purpose of all human life is to glorify God? And then that meant we conducted our families, finances, homes, businesses, and civic affairs (as well as our churches) to that end?

Of course, we can't do these things via our own striving. Unregenerate man isn't capable of moving beyond his own sinfulness to any consistent state of selflessness, and we can probably debate whether the unregenerate would even want to if they could.

But those of us who do already have the Holy Spirit actively at work in our lives can do at least some of these things. There are estimates that only about 10 percent of those who identify as Christians have a Biblical worldview. About two hundred million Americans currently claim to be Christians. Ten percent of that number would be twenty million people. Only three states—California,

Texas, and Florida—are currently home to that many people or more. Maybe it's just me, but I kinda think twenty million people could wreak a lot of heavenly havoc.

We know in the Bible what God can do with just Gideon's three hundred or Christ's twelve apostles. Imagine what He could do with twenty million sold out to glorify Him as He alone is worthy?

There were only 102 Pilgrims who set sail on the *Mayflower* for the New World. There were only fifty-six signers to the Declaration of Independence. These were the two groups that divine providence used to give birth to the greatest country ever.

Don't tell me twenty million people couldn't be used to save it.

Group discussion question:

1. What are you prepared to do?

About the Author

Steve Deace hosts a daily show on BlazeTV. He's also the author of several books, including the number one bestseller *Faucian Bargain: The Most Powerful and Dangerous Bureaucrat in American History*. His 2016 book, *A Nefarious Plot*, will soon be adapted into a motion picture. He lives in Iowa with his wife and family.

Made in United States
Orlando, FL
16 December 2021